Barmy Army

by
Alan Allsop

A Twisted Psyche publication

For Steve

Contents

Introduction

This book is about being a football hooligan back in the days when it was relatively harmless fun. Some may say it was never harmless fun but we'll have to agree to differ on that.

Forget the images you've seen on the TV or in the press with hundreds of youths rampaging all over Europe. This story recalls the tale of a small group of lads spending days and nights out in unfamiliar towns before, during and after football matches in the late seventies and early eighties. Getting into scrapes and getting up to daft tricks. Fighting? Yes there was plenty of fighting, far too much to cover in detail, and while some of the battles are recalled here I hope this book conveys more about the characters involved and what went on around those fights than the fights alone.

This book recalls actual events, although one or two of the minor details may be a bit muddled. Time does that to memories and there are more than thirty years between the first event mentioned and the last words going down on paper, so exactly who did or said what may have got a little confused here and there. Therefore if I credit the wrong person with the wrong words or actions occasionally I apologise but it should not detract from the story.

The majority of the action took place in the lower divisions. I can't help that, that's where my team were. If we were in a higher division things may or may not have been the same, who knows?

To protect the 'guilty' I have changed the names but those who were there may think they recognise their character and hopefully remember the good times we had along the way. To those who weren't there, to those who have only heard the rumours, hearsay and legends I hope this will enlighten and maybe even amuse because we did have a lot of laughs along the way.

This does not set out to be one of those books where the author is desperately trying to prove he was the best or the hardest. He knows he wasn't. It is simply an account of what took place from someone who was there. I seek no glory, I have few regrets. I simply wish to tell it how it was for me.

I was employed, I was fairly well paid, I was pretty intelligent even if I say so myself, I came from a solid family background, and for a while at least I was a bloody good football hooligan.

Why was I a hooligan? What caused me to become one of those youths portrayed in the media as the lowest of the low? What was the problem with society that made youths like me become scum? There was no problem. Stuff all the fancy psychology and sociology; I didn't become a hooligan to rebel against poverty and poor housing. I didn't do it because I saw no future except long-term unemployment. I didn't do it as an act of political rebellion against the government of the day. I did it for the buzz. I did it because it gave me a high no drugs could give. I did it because inside, all young men are warriors and I'd been presented with an arena in which to test my skill against others. I did it to people who were trying to do the same to me and on the whole those who got hurt got hurt because they were looking for it, and sometimes they came off worst. It was accepted as an occupational hazard.

I operated in a time before the mobile phone, before the Internet. This was when things weren't '*organised*'. We didn't need a website to set up a brawl. If we were playing Millwall we all went to Millwall and Millwall were there waiting for us. We didn't need technology to tell us that.

We weren't all Neanderthals. We had our code. There was no kudos in fighting the weak or the defenceless. On the whole it was toe to toe unarmed combat between like-minded groups of youths. If you weren't looking for trouble you usually didn't get it. On a few occasions I even saw full-blown riots stop while some old lady or young mother was ushered out of the way before the scrap would start again. It was simple, it was basic and it was mostly fun. When it started to change I got out.

For a while I was a face. For a while I gave the ball a right old kick. For a while, before it all started getting fucking stupid I had some bloody good times. Sure there were times when I wondered what it was all about and why I was getting involved at all, but at other times I was 'The Man' and I revelled in it.

Chapter One

JOINING THE BIG BOYS

Blades 3 - 2 West ham
10th March 1976

Hull City 2 – 3 Blades
31st December 1977

Brighton 2 – 0 Blades
17th March 1979

I was a Blade. I followed the Blades and I fought for the Blades.

I started going to the football regularly when the Blades were a pretty good side. I was brought up on Alan Woodward, Geoff Salmons and Billy Dearden. I remember Eddie Colquhoun marshalling the defence, Trevor Hockey snapping at heels for the ball and of course Tony Currie the best player I ever saw and am ever likely to see play for the Blades.

I was ten when we were promoted to Division One, I was eleven when the Blades briefly stood shoulder to shoulder with Man United at the top of the league. I was hooked, and as I entered my teens I began to notice there were other battles going on as the football teams played each other. I was fascinated as the gangs of youths who stood behind the goal fought with each other to see who got to stand in the best position. I felt proud when the supporters of the Blades held their ground and I felt ashamed when, as often happened in those days, our boys were moved on by the likes of Man United and Leeds. As I got a bit older *I* wanted to become one of those boys. *I* wanted to defend our kop. *I* wanted to make sure we got to stand behind the goal.

I'd been getting involved on the fringes of the hooligan scene since I was about fourteen. In that time I'd seen our crew develop from a pretty shoddy mob that got chased off our kop quite often, especially by the big clubs of the time, into a quite respectable crew with a growing reputation.

I suppose the turning point, as I saw it, was the year Leeds came expecting the usual easy walk onto our kop and got run off it before half time. Up until that game Leeds had pissed on our kop at will and we had to suffer the embarrassment of watching those wankers with their flags and banners cheering their bunch of big headed prima donnas on from the end that was supposed to be our stronghold. The lasting memory of that night for me was looking up towards the back of the kop where the Leeds scum were assembled and seeing the silhouetted shape of one of our most respected boys jumping over a segregating fence and wading in as more of our lot followed. The Leeds mob had not been used to opposition, due to the huge numbers they took away, and they shit themselves and did a runner as our

2

crew poured over the fence. To this day they have not been back on our kop.

Another turning point for me personally was when West Ham came early in 1976. They had a well-respected crew and the reputation of some of their top boys had reached right across the country. For this game they came on our kop and got well sorted out and I was involved properly for the first time. They were assembling a crew to the side of our main mob getting ready to have a pop. What they didn't know was that we had seen this tactic before and we had a secondary mob, of which I was one, assembled in the far corner keeping a low profile while they were in position. While their attention was on the main crew we attacked from the rear and they were taken by surprise and caught in a pincer movement. There I was on the front line going toe to toe with West Ham at fifteen years old and coming out on top. The Blades won the match 3-2 after being behind and when the third goal went in me and my mate ran on the pitch and were subsequently thrown out of the ground. As we wandered along Shoreham Street looking for a way back in we saw a few West Ham fans including a big black lad fighting with some of our fans who were leaving early. As we continued to look for a way back into the ground a couple of other youths came towards us. "Be careful if you go that way." I said "There's a big black lad kicking the shit out of anyone who comes near him".

"What, you mean Cass?" said one of the youths, who turned out to be more West Ham fans and they both took up a stance ready to rumble. Just in time a copper moved in and split us up. Now I don't know how many other Hammers there are called Cass but I would guess that we may have had just had a glimpse of a young Mr Pennant in action.

Unfortunately as our crew got better the Blades got worse and at the end of that season we were relegated to Division Two where the opposition weren't as worthy but I began to look at it as a good apprenticeship for when the big teams came back. I became more and more involved with our hooligan element, who had christened themselves 'The Shoreham Republican Army' before simplifying it to 'The Barmy Army'. At first I was just involved at the home matches but, once I'd passed my driving test and bought a car, I gradually started to have a pop at some away grounds as well. In one year taking on the kops of Oldham, Hull and Notts County with four or five mates and moving them on enough to encourage larger parts of our crew to get across the pitch with backup. These teams were all relative lightweights but it was good training and I was starting to get noticed by some of the top boys.

The only lowlight of this time was at Hull where, after having a go at their kop but then getting moved on by the coppers, I got my first arrest when, later in the game, some twat of a copper pulled me from the crowd. The copper took me round the back of the stand and asked me if I wanted to be arrested or to receive a good kicking. I opted for the good kicking which he and his mate gave me, then the bastard arrested me anyway. Later he made up a load of bollocks in court resulting in a £75 fine. I was well fucked off at the time but as this turned out to be my only conviction I suppose it was cheap when you consider all the times I got away with it.

Then in March 1979 at an away match at Brighton I received my first 'cap'. Not literally but that's how it seemed to me at the time. Brighton being a long way and my car of the time being a bit unreliable I, and a few of my mates, had gone by supporters' club coach, a bit naff I know, but it was cheap. We were at the Goldstone Ground and the local police were fucking about with a ludicrous tactic that was meant to reduce trouble at the match. What they were doing was pulling out fans who were threatening to get out of order and placing them in the midst of the opposite crew on a one for one basis. I suppose the theory behind this was that if anyone started fighting, the crowd on the opposite side would take reprisals on the few boys who were placed amongst them. A sort of a Mexican standoff, so to speak. The trouble with this tactic was that it presumed that football hooligans gave a shit. It also presumed that the small group of fans amongst the larger group of opposition fans were scared when outnumbered. Neither of these presumptions was true in our case.

We were on the side terrace adjacent to the Brighton kop and I had been lifted by the cops after shouting abuse at the Brighton mob at the other side of a fence and, along with five or six other lads, had been exchanged with a similar amount of Brighton fans. So there we were on the Brighton kop among maybe two hundred of their lot, most of whom were just hangers on, and just over the fence were a small group of Brighton fans in the middle of our travelling crew maybe five hundred strong, half of whom were up for it. Protecting each group of 'alien' fans were two coppers. The maths now starts to kick in and it's not hard to work out what happens next.

Seeing that our lads weren't worried about how we could handle ourselves and were about to have a pop at the Brighton fans, which would inevitably result in the Brighton mob having a go at us, I decided to take matters into my own hands. Pre-emptive strike I think is the term. I couldn't be arsed to wait for an attack so I just waded in to the Brighton kop and the others with me followed suit. All fucking hell let loose as the rest of our crew waded into the Brighton fans among them and then a few started jumping the fence to assist us. The coppers were not prepared and had to retreat and reform before eventually restoring order some five minutes later, an eternity in football battling terms.

Anyway this action got me really noticed and when I had been put back on the right end after the order was restored I was approached by one of the lads from the Barmy Army and invited to join them on their coach which was heading for London after the match for a night in the west end. I always remember his words.

"You can come, you're solid, but just you, not your mates."

This told me I had taken the step up; I was the face in our small group. I was happy to take up the offer and, in my eyes, enter the big league so off to London it was. We were dropped off on the edge of Trafalgar Square and were due to be picked up at midnight in Whitehall. In between we were to do the rounds of Charring Cross and Soho, get plenty of beer down our necks and see what came our way.

There was no real trouble early on as most of the people in the pubs we visited were tourists up west for a show or whatever. So we had a few drinks and a bit of a laugh and the mood grew quite relaxed. We marched round London like we owned the place and when we came across the occasional crew of fans from the other clubs that had been playing in London that day we saw them off with little opposition. It felt good. I picked up a few tips about blagging beer and food for free and later on I witnessed what remains one of the all-time great sights of my away travels when one of our crew was struck by a sudden desire for something to eat. Spotting a shop which sold nothing but roast chickens he decided to chance his arm at thieving one. This seemed a quite easy prospect as there were freshly roasted chickens fastened all around the window and door frames aimed at enticing customers in to buy the goods. This lad, seeing the prospect of a free nosh, simply reached around the door jamb grabbed a chicken and ran like fuck down the street with his catch. What he hadn't noticed was that the chickens in the window were all fastened together on a string. As he ran away he was followed by a line of thirty roast chickens bouncing down the road and chased by an angry proprietor wielding a meat cleaver while all his mates were rolling about laughing.

As the night wore on our numbers began thinning as was usual. Some lads got left behind each time we moved or some would splinter off towards a favourite haunt away from the main crew. It always leaves you a bit vulnerable but trying to keep a large group together when the threat seems small is always difficult. Being a newcomer to the group I stuck by the faces I knew and could trust to stand if it went tits up and we did several pubs without much incident before settling down in one we had taken a liking to ready to make a session of it. The night was turning out to be a good one.

Shortly after that it all went shit shaped. Half of our remaining crew decided to move down towards Trafalgar Square while the other half, me included, stayed to finish our drinks and get ready to watch Match of the Day on the pub TV, arranging to meet up back at the coach. Although that cut each group down to about a dozen in number we reckoned that was enough for any situation that might arise. We hadn't figured on two hundred Nottingham Forest fans fresh from winning the League Cup. The Forest mob had been prowling the West End most of the evening looking for action but finding very little mainly due to our paths not crossing earlier. What they had succeeded in doing was attracting the attention of the Metropolitan Police. They were now being followed by several units of anti-riot police and had been infiltrated by about twenty plain clothes officers. These were the forerunners of the many anti hooligan units that were to develop up and down the country over the coming years.

This marauding mob arrived in Trafalgar Square at the same time as the half of our crew who had just left us at the pub. Hearing the chanting and singing coming from the other side of the square our mob started shouting and singing back and headed towards the noise expecting to find a similar sized crew to have a pop at. What they actually found was not good at all. As they squared up they were taken aback by the size of the mob facing them but having committed to the battle they had no choice but to follow through and so they waded in. What happened next was relayed to those of us who had stayed in the pub by one of the few who had managed to come out of the mess relatively un-scathed. More by luck than judgement he had gone the opposite way around one of the statues hoping to get stuck in from behind and had been missed by the sudden influx of batten wielding police who appeared from nowhere within seconds of the first punch being thrown. Unlike the coppers at Brighton these coppers were sorted like no others we had previously come across and had managed to stop the fighting, disperse the crowd and nick most of our mob and an equal number of Forest fans within a couple of minutes.

We decided to get out of the pub and find out what was happening for ourselves and were confronted by scenes reminiscent of a disaster movie. On every corner stood two or three coppers dressed in full riot gear. Police cars and vans sped up and down the road lights blazing and sirens wailing. What people remained on the street seemed to be hurrying on their way to wherever, flitting from shadow to shadow, hoping to avoid the attention of anyone who might be looking. Any group of more than three or four people were being stopped and lined up against the wall and searched and anyone found carrying something the police didn't like were being loaded into vans and carted away.

"Fuck this," I said to a lad called Lenny "let's get out of here."

So Lenny and me peeled away from the rest of our crew and slid into a bar fifty yards up the road while the rest of our lot split into small groups and dispersed. Even then some of them got pulled by the cops and banged up in vans.

This was the first time we had come across such heavy tactics from the police and we were taken back by it, not really knowing what to do next. We had about two hours to go before the coach would arrive in Whitehall to pick us up and we were now down to the two of us in a hostile environment. We knew that as well as the coppers there could be any number of small gangs looking for people like us as easy targets and we would have to be careful. Lenny suggested we try and team up with a few more of our lot who had escaped the net of the coppers and he reckoned that any stragglers would probably head for The Cockney Pride in Piccadilly as that was apparently our normal rendezvous point when we were in London.

We could see there was still a great deal of activity in Trafalgar Square so we took a route around the outer edge on the opposite side of the road that surrounds the square. Just as we thought we had got clear of the police activity we came across another problem. Three Forest fans stood on the footpath just outside the entrance to a big stone building looking back across the square. It looked as though they had escaped the main affray like we had and were hanging around wondering what to do next. When they spotted us I could see they were quickly trying to figure out who we were. We could have been fellow fans, tourists, cockneys or even with the police, they couldn't tell because unlike them we wore no colours to identify us to other parties. One of them stepped out and barred our way.

"Where you heading cockney?" he asked Lenny.

Big mistake. It turns out Lenny didn't like cockneys; Lenny especially didn't like being taken for a cockney; Lenny stuck the nut on the Forest fan sending him to the ground clutching his nose. The other two were game and immediately set about us, these were good lads there were no preliminaries, no words of warning, no posturing, straight in. I was faced with a big mean looking bastard who charged at me swinging and kicking. As I swerved to avoid a flailing boot I caught a blow high on my head from a wild swing. I took a step back to clear my head and found myself with my back against a lamppost. Before I had fully recovered he was onto me again lining me up for a good kick in the balls. I instinctively jumped out of the way just before he connected with a boot that would have had me singing soprano for a long time. I got out of the way just in time but the offending boot was committed and connected hard against the lamppost. The big bastard let out a yell and grabbed for his foot, which was probably broken. I saw my chance and charged headlong into the hobbling hooligan sending him sprawling across the footpath. I then stepped towards him and swung my steel toe capped shoe into his body with the same sort of force that he had aimed at me. I must have connected just right as I could actually hear the wind rush from his lungs and he made a horrible sickly noise that I will remember forever.

I looked around and saw Lenny grappling with the other Forest fan and from the corner of my eye saw four coppers running across the road towards us.

"Run." I called to Lenny and set off around the first corner like a bat out of hell. Lenny was fast on his feet and soon caught up with me. We ran like mad not knowing where we were heading, not pausing to look if we were still being chased, we knew we were, coppers don't give up as easily as that. Now totally lost I dashed down a small alley and Lenny followed. Another alley led off this one and as I turned into it I spotted a group of large bins. Without a pause I threw myself up and into the first bin and lay in the rubbish trying to get my breath as my lungs demanded air. Within a few seconds I could hear the sound of the coppers coming into the alley within feet of where I lay. I held my breath so as not to make any noise and my lungs felt as though they would burst. The coppers rushed straight past and out of the alley but I stayed put amongst the stinking rubbish for about five minutes expecting them to return and find me at any time. Eventually I decided the coast must be clear and I clambered out of the bin. I was now in London, split up from my crew, and over an hour away from our midnight rendezvous with the coach in Whitehall.

I first had to find out where I was so after brushing myself down the best I could I came out of the alley and wandered about a bit until I found a place I recognised which in this case was The Mall. I didn't fancy my chances of finding any of our lot in any of the pubs back around the square, and I figured that there might still be a heavy police presence so I decided to wander down towards Buckingham Palace and give myself time to think. The Mall at that time of night is a completely different place to The Mall in the daytime, where there were normally hundreds of tourists wandering about taking in the sights there was now just the odd person scurrying past not wanting to make eye contact. I noticed a tramp picking through the litter and wondered if he had started out running around with a group of youths thinking he was a 'face'. I was sure that some of our crew would probably end up in a similar predicament, hungry, homeless and probably having spent some time inside. I was also sure that I was not going there, I would get out before that happened..... maybe.

That said I still had to get to the coach and make it home. I made my way back towards Whitehall and as I got into Trafalgar Square I bumped into some of our crew who filled me in with details of what had happened to them after we got split up. As we walked down Whitehall more of our lot arrived and stories were exchanged and it seemed that everyone had the same sort of tale to tell involving scuffles, the police and chases around London. Some had come off best others had got a bit of a kicking but that's the nature of the game. It turns out that about twenty had been arrested and taken away by the police during the night so we were a bit lighter on numbers than when we came. I thought about those who had been locked up and thought there but for a bit of luck go I.

The penalties for football hooligans were starting to increase dramatically. Gone were the days when you could get away with a £10 fine and a slapped wrist. Magistrates were now dishing out fines in the hundreds of pounds and tagging community service orders on for good measure. There was even talk of prison for the worst offenders. I wanted none of that.

With this thought still in my mind I waded straight into the next incident. Some of the lads had relayed a tale of how they had been attacked by a group of Norwich fans of all people. These were considered to be a bit of a joke and were not rated by anyone in the football world but that night about a dozen of them had come across two of our lads after they had been split up. Seizing the opportunity to use their superior numbers they had proceeded to give our lot a bit

10

of a kicking. This was probably a first and if the story got out then our reputation could be severely damaged.

Anyway we were sat on the coach in Whitehall waiting for the last of our crew to arrive when suddenly one of the lads who had taken a beating started shouting,

"That's them, that's the bastards." He cried as a group of youths walked right past our coach. I was sat near the front of the coach and instinctively jumped off and ran at them. I was followed by about six more of our crew. We chased them across Whitehall and I managed to corner one against a large black hoarding. As he backed against the boards I ran in and landed a sweet right hander right on his chin knocking his head back into the boards with a bang. To my horror a door opened up at the end of the hoarding and several policemen started spilling out. It turned out that this was a police cabin where the old bill were on standby in case of any bother around Downing Street and other government offices and I was now being pursued by some of the Metropolitan Constabularies best. Fortunately it was a short distance back to the bus and the first coppers out had taken the easy option and grabbed the nearest people regardless of whether they had committed any offence. This gave me a chance to make it back onto the bus and hide among thirty similarly dressed lads. Two coppers came on board the coach but, seeing the difficulty in identifying me among this crowd, given they had only got a fleeting glance of my back, and probably because they didn't want the paperwork at that hour they ordered the driver to leave and took no further action. So we headed back home without those who had been arrested and without two of those who had jumped off the bus with me and had run away from the coach when the police showed up; que sera.

Anyway this trip confirmed me as sound in the eyes of those that mattered and I was offered an open invitation to join them on any of their away trips. I felt proud that they had received me as one of their own. However I preferred the freedom of travelling independently to the away games as a rule. It allowed you much more choice of where you went and when you went and you were much less likely to be rounded up by the police and herded into the ground hours before kick-off so I thanked them for the offer but explained that I normally travelled by car but that I would be glad to join up with them when they arrived at the games. I was now officially a face.

Chapter 2

THE FIRST OF THE WILD WEEKENDS

Blackburn 2 – 0 Blades
7th April 1979

Now I was *'One of the lads'* I wanted more and more of the notoriety it brought and I was looking for ways of getting more action. I'd been doing the away matches in my car and had recently bought a little van, mainly for the options it offered for laying down in the back, if you know what I mean. Then during a drinking session before a game someone suggested making some away games a weekend thing. You know, go Friday night, do the town, sleep in the van and do the game on Saturday. Sometimes we'd come straight back after the game others we'd have the Saturday night on the town and come back Sunday. It seemed like a good idea so I thought why not give it a try. It was after the first of the long ones that I realised that we would have to get a much better set up if we were going to come back at all.

Blackburn Rovers away. Not much of a threat, usually good for a scuffle outside and then home for tea. This time it went much as anticipated and the night before in a small town pub on the Lancashire side of the Pennines had been just another night out with the lads. No hassle and no trouble getting to sleep in the back of a cold Bedford van with almost a gallon of best bitter down my neck.

On the Saturday there was no trouble before the game or inside the ground. Blackburn was a place where it had always proved difficult to get on the kop. The local plod seemed to be able to smell a Yorkshire man from fifty yards and we always seemed to get recognised and shoved onto the away end. Outside the ground after the game, which we lost two nil, we were escorted en-mass to the coach park regardless of whether we had actually travelled by coach and there had been a couple of clashes with the hot pot brigade on the way.

There was a great incident as we were marching back to the coach park when during a clash with a few Blackburn lads a police horse was drafted in. As the mounted policeman tried to restore order his horse nodded its head, banging against one of our lads shoulders. The lad who was looking the other way and had not seen the horse thought that he was being attacked by the Lancastrians and turned around swinging his fists at his assailant. I don't know who was the most surprised, him or the horse as he landed a big right hook on the horse's nose.

Once the coppers left us at the coaches we made our way back to the van and joined the queue of traffic leaving Blackburn. While in the queue we spotted some Blackburn fans on a corner throwing stones at our coaches so we took a couple of left turns, parked the van and ran at them from behind giving them a good kicking as we were cheered on by our fans on the passing coaches.

It was on the Saturday night after the game that we hit the first snags. Most of our fans had been escorted out of Blackburn, as was usual in most towns for away fans at the time, so we didn't want to hang around Blackburn where there would be too many home fans on the lookout for us. Blackpool was appealing but in the wrong direction and at the wrong time of the year. Manchester was the right way, but four Yorkshire lads in that particular city were more likely to attract a beating than a turd attracts flies. Then someone suggested Oldham and no one said no, so Oldham it was. What could go wrong in Oldham? I mean Oldham was where we'd taken their kop with ease for the previous two seasons. Oldham was where they would run like fuck from anyone and everyone wasn't it?

We were to find out that this was the Oldham where they employ martial arts experts as night-club bouncers who'd throw troublemakers downstairs as soon as look at them. This was the Oldham where a so called mate fucks off at the first sign of bother and leaves you to kick your way out of a back ally ambush set up by some pretty handy locals.

I suppose, looking back, that it was the extra three or four shorts at the night-club that led to the lapse in concentration that got us into the jam in the first place. I'd normally sense a situation coming up and handle it before the opposition had time to get organised, or plan a hasty retreat if the odds were too great. I'm not talking about bottling out, but when the odds are stacked way two high only a fucking idiot sticks around for a certain kicking. I preferred to back off and hit them in smaller groups later. But this was Oldham for fucks sake and we were out for a laugh and looking forward to who knows what when the clubs turned out.

Normally I would have been aware of the number of blokes in the club getting fewer and fewer and my senses would have told me all was not well. But this night the combination of the drink and the fact that this was '*only Oldham*' distracted me from my usual cautious scanning of the crowd and constant appraisal of the situation. I suppose there was also the fact that after my recent escapades I was getting a bit complacent and starting to think I was invincible. If Oldham taught me nothing else it taught me not to let my guard down.

Malcolm was one of the crew on that trip. He had been to the same school as me but mixed in different circles. We had only started hanging around together after we had left school. He was a big strong lad, six feet high, three feet across the shoulders and completely off his trolley. He worked as a steel erector for a large construction company earning a fortune for risking his neck at stupid heights walking on four inch wide girders as though he was strolling in the park. He had come on a couple of previous trips and had always talked a good fight. I had him down as a good bet to hold his own in a scuffle even though I thought he was a bit too mouthy to keep out of trouble when a bit of cunning might be required. This night it was Malcolm that lit the fuse. Malcolm came over to me and said he thought we should go on the dance floor and inject a bit of punk style into the boring atmosphere. I knew what he meant, we were all still living in the aftermath of the punk era and this club was definitely more Saturday Night Fever than Never Mind the Bollocks. Anyway I told Malcolm that if he wanted to go and jump up and down like he was busting for a piss then that was up to him but I was staying where I was. In truth I had never been a great one for dancing I had probably only danced three times in my life and all three were drunken smooches that ended up in me getting dizzy and a girl getting her toes trampled. So I preferred to stick to the side lines and keep my eye on where the trouble might come from so I was always one step ahead. Except on this night I wasn't.

There were four of us on the trip, Malcolm as mentioned, Benny, Billy, and me Benny was the younger but bigger brother of another old schoolmate. He was a strapping lad of six feet tall who had been a heavy beer drinker since he was thirteen. He always looked like he could handle himself but usually got too pissed to manage it. Not a runner though which counts for a lot. Billy was a lad a bit younger than the rest of us who I didn't know from Adam but Malcolm had said he was sound. Billy looked the part, he was just under six feet tall and well-built but to me he had this aura about him that just said '*wanker*'. I'd had my doubts when I first saw Billy. These doubts grew stronger when during a conversation on the way to the game it turns out that his only experience of footballs other attraction was watching somebody getting a kicking at Forest, and calling a policeman a tit head as he sped past on a coach.

Finally of course there was me, I stood at exactly six feet tall, was slim but not thin with good upper body strength although I had never worked out, it just came naturally. What I did have and I did work on, and what usually gave me an edge, was the ability to quickly weigh up a situation and decide how to handle it. I also had the sometimes frightening ability to dive in and do something apparently reckless while others were still thinking over their next move. On the whole this gave me the element of surprise and generally got me out of more trouble than it got me into. I did quite often look back and wonder '*why the fuck did I do that*' but I was young and if you can't be a bit mental when you're young when can you? Anyway there we were the four of us in a nightclub in Oldham about to get a bloody good hiding.

The club was a smallish place set over a department store. There was an illuminated central dance floor made up of different coloured squares lit from underneath. Each square would flash on and off at random, very seventies and frankly if I had stood on it for more than thirty seconds it would have done my head in. Immediately around the dance floor were a number of small circular tables each surrounded by chairs or stools to sit on. At the perimeter of the room there was fixed seating against the walls all covered in burgundy draylon to go with the flock wallpaper and red curtains. Apart from the dance floor and the bar the only other lighting was from a series of very low wattage lights suspended above each of the circular tables giving off just about enough light to see what you were drinking and not much more. The whole atmosphere fell somewhere between Indian restaurant and Hollywood brothel. One full wall was taken up by the bar and a small serving hatch where those who wanted food could get what were known as basket meals which were the in thing at the time. These consisted of fifteen greasy chips and a chicken drumstick, probably with a dose of salmonella thrown in. All for the price of a terrace ticket at Arsenal. On the opposite wall was the main entrance and to one side of the entrance the ladies and gents toilets and a cloakroom. A third wall was completely covered with fixed seating as was the fourth wall with the exception of a door marked '*Fire Exit*'. One hundred and fifty people would have had the place bursting at the seams but when we arrived it was only just over half full and recently there seemed to be even fewer people around.

It was in a corner where two runs of fixed seating met that I had chosen to sit, while my brain was still in survival mode, so that I had a good view of what was going on and no one was going to come up behind me and crack me over the head. As was usual in this type of situation we would have a pint or two together then keep splitting up and having a wander around doing our own thing but meeting up every few minutes to check what was happening, always keeping an eye on each other's backs.

Benny was at one of the circular tables between me and the dance floor with a girl he had brought from the pub we had been in earlier and another girl she knew who had been in the club when we arrived. While he was busy trying to chat up these two I had noticed he was also doing his best to try and pull one of the clubs attempts at a bunny girl, a slightly too fat teenage glass collector in a black corset with a bit of cotton wool stuck to her arse. I was just thinking how it would all end in grief and wondering where the fuck Billy was when my attention was distracted by Malcolm on the dance floor. I had been vaguely aware of him doing the pogo to Gloria Gaynor, which looked stupid but was otherwise doing no harm, but now he had started jumping from square to square as each one lit up knocking people left right and centre. As my brain started to pull back into gear I gave a nod to Benny whose thoughts must have been at about the same stage in the '*Oh Oh here comes trouble*' process as mine because he had just stopped billing and cooing to the two birds at his table and was doing a swift reccy of the room to get his bearings.

Two bouncers had appeared from nowhere and were leading Malcolm off the dance floor. Even in my slightly drunken state I was immediately aware of two more on the main door, one on the emergency exit and two of the bar staff who had stopped serving and were stood at either end of the bar ready to wade in if needed, I was impressed. I just caught sight of the cowardly figure of Billy sliding out of the main entrance as Benny stood up and started heading towards Malcolm. I followed as casually as I could, trying not to attract attention and making sure we were not all in a tight spot that would make us a sitting target for anyone who decided to have a pop.

As I was quickly scanning the room for potential threats and possible weapons in case it all went pear shaped I noticed that there wasn't a single tough looking bloke in the place. I recall thinking it was funny and I could have sworn there were at least half a dozen handy looking types around when we came in. Never mind less chance of a riot.

As I approached the two bouncers holding Malcolm, I could overhear Benny asking them to take it easy and pleading Malcolm's case not to be thrown out. I manoeuvred around the group so that while Malcolm, Benny and myself had both bouncers in sight each of them could only focus on two out of the three of us at a time, everything right so far. It seemed as though Benny's pleas must have been working because the smaller one of the bouncers released his grip on Malcolm and seemed to relax, his shoulders sagging and he seemed to visibly shrink by two inches. I chose this moment to intervene and made the mistake of moving a step closer. We were now stood in a tight triangle around the small bouncer with the bigger one still holding Malcolm. None of the other bouncers had moved. We seemed to be in the boss seat.

I started to say "What's the problem?" but before the words had come out the little one swiftly brought his elbow back and upwards into my face sending me reeling backwards. As I stumbled I can remember seeing it all in slow motion, like you do in a car crash. The little one then thrust forward with the arm that had just pole axed me and hit Benny square on the jaw. In the same instant he threw a sideways blow with the other arm bringing the back of his clenched fist hard against Malcolm's nose, instantly spreading it across his face and sending a splattering of blood all over anyone in the vicinity. As I stumbled backwards my hand caught the back of a chair which I used to steady myself. I then picked up the chair and swung it at the little bastard who had just elbowed me. Got you I thought as the chair arched round towards his tightly cropped hairline. Just as I thought the chair was about to strike him he suddenly dropped to the floor spinning and kicking, knocking my legs out from under me sending me dropping onto my back and knocking the wind from my lungs. To add insult to injury, or maybe that should be injury to insult, the chair which I had swung at the bouncer and which had been knocked from my grip landed on top of me. The only good news was that as the little bloke had kicked my legs out from under me Malcolm had swung a leg out and caught him full in the face taking him out of the proceedings for the next few minutes. Spotting his chance, Benny had then picked up an ashtray from one of the tables and cracked the other bouncer over the head causing him to release Malcolm and drop to his knees clutching his skull. This whole fracas lasted only a few seconds.

As I got to my feet I was suddenly fully sober and instantly aware of more bouncers heading across the club towards us. Fortunately the combination of tables, chairs and fascinated onlookers hindered their progress for just long enough for me to shout "fire exit" at Benny and Malcolm and make a dash for the small door in the wall which was manned by a bouncer who had never moved through the whole rumpus. Benny was the first there and strangely the bouncer didn't wade in but simply opened the door as though he was a commissionaire at a posh hotel. Benny fell for it and rushed past but as he did the bouncer caught him by the shirt and spun him around against the wall of the small landing on the other side of the door. This landing was about six feet square and had a flight of stairs heading down from the far corner. As Malcolm and I followed Benny and the bouncer onto the landing I could see two more bouncers starting to run up the stairs towards us. My brain did some quick calculations and came up with figures that I did not like at all. There were two bouncers on the stairs one on the landing, as well as four fit and two injured and mad as fuck coming from behind. That

20

made nine on to three in a confined space with no witnesses. At best a visit to casualty was looming.

Without any further conscious thought I rushed virtually head first down the stairs in a potentially suicidal dive towards the onrushing bouncers sending us all hurtling to the bottom of the stairs in a tangle of arms and legs like some cartoon avalanche. As we hit the floor I landed on top of the bouncers and crashed against the fire exit doors at the bottom of the stairs sending them flying open. As I scrambled out into the cold night air I was quickly followed by Malcolm who trampled all over the two prostrate bouncers putting the finishing touches to a thoroughly good winding and probably a few broken ribs. As we spilled out into what turned out to be an alley about ten feet wide between two tall department stores we spotted a group of large galvanised steel bins on wheels which we quickly dragged over and used to jam the exit doors shut. This would hopefully prevent anyone else following, then grinning to each other we started to head down the alley towards the main street and our escape.

Our grins lasted about five seconds for as we reached the end of the alley we found out where the rest of the locals from the night-club had gone. Forming a circle in the street around the end of the alley were about twenty cocky looking Lancastrians all aged between eighteen and twenty five and most looking like they knew how to dish out a good kicking.

"Fucking hell," said Malcolm "I don't fancy this."

"See the little ginger bastard on the left." I said, quickly weighing up the opposition.

"Yeah." said Malcolm.

"Run at him then keep on going."

So we ran at the little ginger bastard who I'd correctly sussed as a wanker who was just making up the numbers. Ginger promptly shit himself and moved to one side leaving a gap just big enough for me and Malcolm to dash through collecting a couple of glancing but harmless blows on the way through.

21

As we ran I glanced back over my shoulder and saw the sight of twenty of Oldham's finest heading after us in a formation like geese flying south for winter.

"Keep running." I yelled at Malcolm who had also looked back and saw no point in arguing. We must have legged it for a good quarter of a mile through the town centre and when I looked back, although we were still being followed, there had been a definite split in the ranks of those chasing us. Three of the lads were well out in front intent on giving us a pasting and another group of five or six were some way behind, the rest of the mob having given up the chase early on.

Malcolm was tiring and he said, "I can't run much further."

"Good," I said "take the next corner and we'll give them the old shop door surprise."

"Just like Burnley." said Malcolm remembering a previous encounter.

So we swung round the next corner and at once Malcolm ducked into the first shop doorway and hid in the shadows. I ran another fifteen yards and stopped at the side of a phone box. This served to narrow the footpath and make it harder for the following group to surround me. I turned and faced back the way we came just as the first three came running around the corner. As expected they were taken by surprise by the sight of me just stood there waiting for them and they stopped six feet short of me and waited for me to make a move. They should have just waded in, at least they would have got a few blows in before getting theirs, but instead they stood and waited, so to buy just enough time for what we had in mind I said, "This is unfair, three of you and one of me;" I then added "I should go and fetch a couple more if I were you, if you don't want your arses kicked."

I don't know what they must have thought of the situation, this lad on his own outnumbered in a strange town fronting them up and grinning like a Cheshire cat. What I could see and they couldn't was Malcolm coming up behind them with a stick that he must have found in the shop doorway and was just about to bring crashing over the head of the biggest of our foes. As the stick crashed over his head and he collapsed in a heap I immediately waded in to the one nearest

22

the phone box swinging like a man possessed and catching him square on the jaw with a big right haymaker leaving him sat on the pavement with his back to the phone box gurgling like a baby. The other one, now outnumbered and faced with Malcolm holding what remained of a broken stick, decided he'd had enough and set off running back the way he came and probably all the way home. The rest of the chasing pack must have either given up the chase before they got to the corner we had turned, or seen their mate running back in terror and called it a day. Either way they never appeared and Malcolm and me got back our breath and our bearings and made our way back to where we had left the van.

When we got back to the van surprise surprise there was Billy unmarked unflustered and greeting us with a cheery "Hello lads, what's up? Where's Benny?"

Before I had chance to give him some what's fucking up, the *'Where's Benny'* bit sank in.

"Fucking hell," I said "he's still in there."

We quickly jumped into the van and as I drove towards the night-club Malcolm released the two catches of the false floor I had installed in the van. Under the false floor panel was a baseball bat, a cut down pick shaft and a leather-covered cosh that I had stashed away for just such emergencies. I didn't like going tooled up but sometimes you had to have an edge when the odds were too high and retreat was not an option. I parked around the corner from the club and jumped out of the van. Adrenaline was pumping through our veins and our minds were set on revenge, when out of nowhere appeared Benny wearing no shirt and only one shoe. Blood was streaming down his chest from his nose and mouth and he was singing, "We are the reds, we are the reds, we are, we are, we are the reds."

When he saw us he shouted, "What a night, did we give them a right kicking or what?" before promptly collapsing on the pavement in front of us. I looked at Malcolm, Malcolm looked at me and together we both said "Home" and gathered up Benny, Billy and the *'tools'* and got back in the van and headed for home.

As we drove over the Pennines and the adrenaline wore off the aches and pains started. Malcolm tried to make the swollen lump in the middle of his face look like something resembling a nose again. Benny sat in a daze and Billy cowered silently in the back corner of the van painfully aware of how he'd bottled out and left the rest of us up against even higher odds than we already were.

During the journey home I discussed the night's events with Malcolm and we spoke of how lucky we'd been and how in future we must be better prepared for that sort of situation and to myself I was already making plans for bigger and better things.

Chapter 3

THE CRAZY DAISY

Blades 5 – 1 Notts County
10th April 1979

Cambridge Utd 1 – 0 Blades
5th May 1979

Between matches we used to meet at the Crazy Daisy in the centre of Sheffield. It wasn't much of a place on the face of it but it stayed open while two in the morning, had no dress code and played the right sort of music which was a mixture of rock, punk and new wave stuff and none of that wishy washy soul crap that refused to leave the charts.

The Daisy was a basement bar that had previously been a Bier Keller and still retained the same furniture and decor which consisted of bare wooden tables and benches. It had vaulted ceilings and rough plastered walls. The main part of the club was a long thin room with a small dance floor opposite what looked like a church pulpit which was where the resident DJ would spin his records from 9pm until 2am, punch ups and police raids permitting. This layout caused a severe bottle neck for anyone trying to get past when it was busy and a good spot to rub up against the birds that frequented the place, none of whom seemed to mind. The Daisy attracted the sort of girl who went home disappointed if she hadn't been felt up at least once in a night. There was a bar at each end of the room and at the far end the room opened out into a wider space where at lunch times it served as a restaurant and at nights it provided a more comfortable seating area. This part of the club was usually frequented by the druggies who smoked and traded cannabis and could have any questionable substances down the adjacent toilets before any police raiding party could get past the bottleneck.

The Daisy had a reputation as a rough house but we very rarely had any trouble there. This was partly because we had a reputation of being a useful crew and partly because each gang that frequented the club knew that if they caused a fuss and got barred from the Daisy there was nowhere else they could go unless they dressed up like a set of Nancy boys. The New Romantics were the order of the day in most of the other clubs in town and were filled by blokes with big hair and eye liner.

What trouble did occur was usually either individual bust ups that were quickly dealt with by the bouncers or from out of town crews who wandered in by mistake and usually didn't get much more than ten feet past the door. Our crew normally sat at a bench behind the entrance door on a raised area which gave us a good view of what was happening throughout the length of the club and gave us the advantage of height if trouble did start.

Most of the lads used to get into the club just before 10pm, after which time they started charging an entrance fee, but I generally got there about 11pm after I had dropped my regular girlfriend off at home. I suppose I was a bit of a Clark Kent. I held a steady job had a steady girlfriend and did all the normal law abiding stuff day in day out. Then late at night and at football matches I turned in to someone else entirely and the people I mixed with in each segment of my life knew little of what went on in the other. I liked it that way because I knew that while I enjoyed the excitement of the scrapping and the clubbing it wasn't going to last forever and that if I was going to progress to a more comfortable life style as I got older I had to conform to the requirements of the establishment and behave in the appropriate manner. Even if inside I thought they were all a bunch of wankers, they were the wankers making good money, they were the wankers who paid the good money and I was having some of that.

I felt sorry for the bunch of losers who insisted on the spiky red hair, pins through the nose and '*fuck you*' attitude all the time. It was clear to me that the only ones who were going to get fucked were them. So I did my work in the day I tugged the forelock if that was what was necessary and I saw my girlfriend most nights between six and ten. Then I'd shoot down the Daisy and say fuck you to the world while two in the morning. I liked the double life; it offered the best of both worlds I got the kicks that youths around the world seek for fulfilment and at the same time laid the foundations for a comfortable future. For the most part everyone was happy.

It was the Tuesday after the Oldham affair when I next went to the Daisy. We had just beaten Notts County 5-1 at home and I had gone there after the game so I was in earlier than usual. By the time we arrived the tale of Oldham had been going round had been subject to the usual exaggeration. It had almost got to the point where our gang had apparently taken on fifty bouncers and chased the entire population of Oldham out onto Saddleworth moor.

We were greeted by a cheer from the table behind the door and two lads doing impressions of my swan dive, which had according to the legend grown from half a flight of stairs to three floors during the previous two days. The temporary adulation was great and I made the most of the free drinks bought mainly by spotty seventeen year olds who wanted to say that they knew 'the man' but I was concerned about our reputation getting out of hand. It was all right been known as useful, that kept the majority of rivals at arm's length, but once you started getting put up there on a pedestal there were those who saw it as a challenge to have a go and I could do without the hassle. There were also the big boys, the real gangsters who were in a completely different league. They tolerated us while ever we were on a small scale but would rub us out if we started attracting the wrong sort of attention to their territory; people had been known to disappear.

All the lads from the football went to the Daisy and on that night I arrived with Malcolm, Benny and another lad called Jimmy. Jimmy was an old school mate who was hard as nails and reliable to stand and fight against any odds. He was also reliable to try and screw anything slightly resembling a female. Jimmy wasn't the best looking bloke in the world but he had the gift of the gab, a natural curl in his hair and a twinkle in his eye which always seemed to go down well with the ladies. At six feet three he was the biggest of the bunch and he was naturally lean even though he could eat like a pig. He also had a good sense of his own limitations and never set his sights too high. Consequently he always managed to pull something, but fucking hell they were usually pretty rough. Jimmy also had the knack of being able to embroider a tale, so you needed to take some of the things he said with a pinch of salt. The one other thing of note about Jimmy was he had the smelliest feet I had ever come across; he could get straight out of the bath and still do an impression of festering gorgonzola. Even so if I was hand picking a crew for a sticky situation Jimmy would be first on the list every time.

Up until now Jimmy had always resisted invitations to come on our trips, preferring to travel by coach with larger numbers. But now he had started to get details of our exploits he asked if there was any chance of coming on some future trips. I was well chuffed as I was looking for additions to the squad and Jimmy would provide an instant uplift in the quality of the crew that I was trying to put together.

I sat down with Jimmy and had a quiet word in his ear. He eventually agreed that if he was coming along on our trips we needed to take a close look at who else was coming along. We needed to get rid of any muppets and replace them with quality. We also agreed that it wasn't the best idea to let too many other people in on the details of what we got up to, especially as we were picking up rumours of the beginnings of police infiltration of hooligan gangs and the news was beginning to carry items about dawn raids and prison sentences for ringleaders. The last thing I wanted was my name on a computer and ten coppers with growling dogs dragging my family out of bed at five in the morning. So we agreed to stick to people we know, to keep our plans to ourselves and to keep on our guard, which required discipline. We also agreed a code of conduct, which consisted of some formally unwritten rules being confirmed.

We didn't pick fights with fewer numbers than our own, I had been bullied when I was younger and still got well pissed off when I heard people bragging of how three or four of them had beat up one guy.

We didn't start trouble without provocation, there was a great deal of debate as to what constituted provocation. This ranged from spitting in your face to simply being a rival fan but I think we got the idea.

We didn't fight with people who were with their women or youngsters. If they hadn't come for trouble they wouldn't get it.

When someone was out of it we stopped, kicking people when they were down was both cowardly and increased the risk of getting banged up if caught.

We stuck together, we agreed it wasn't always wise to stand and fight when the odds were overwhelming but we either stood as a crew or withdrew as a crew. We also agreed that this meant Billy was out but as Billy had not been seen since Sunday that was a formality anyway.

By the end of the night we had sorted some ideas for future trips and arranged to meet up early for the home game on Saturday. We had also grasped that our temporary fame had not gone unnoticed by the local talent and we had a few eager slappers to choose from.

Jimmy chose, I chose not to. I was never a big one for one night stands. I got my share from my girlfriend and if I pulled while out on the town it was only to prove to myself that I could do it and it would take something really special for me to go any further than a quick kiss and a handful of tit. Besides any bird that was willing to go any further with someone she had only just met was not really the sort of bird I fancied. This attitude had kept me relatively unmolested and totally disease free so far and made the few liaisons I had all the better for it. Jimmy on the other hand couldn't understand my reticence. It was rumoured that he would shag a damp towel if it smelt a bit fishy and that he was regularly up the clap clinic having his japs eye prodded and was thought to have a repeat prescription for penicillin on permanent standby; Well it takes all sorts.

I left Jimmy at 2am relaying the story of how he had single handedly fought off two hundred Millwall fans to two starry eyed, pissed up slag's who believed every word he said. They would both probably have a dose of NSU by the morning, if they hadn't got it already. I went home to my bed and although I didn't realise it then we had just laid the foundations that were going to put us up there as one of the best small gangs among a crew that was to become one of the most respected firms in the country over the next few years.

As it was, the season was drawing to a close and it all ended in grief as we were relegated to the old third division at the last away match at Cambridge. We were doubly sick as Cambridge had no real crew on which to take out our anger. The only bits of action we saw were when a couple of lads climbed one of the floodlights and there was a bit of a battle with the police who were trying to get them down and, after some banter that had been going on with some gardeners in the allotments over the wall immediately behind the away end, we were bombarded with carrots and cabbages! After the match we were let out of the ground and into a field full of cows which was between the ground and the car park. Even though we had just been relegated I had to laugh when one of our top boys lost it and started shouting "What are you fucking looking at you Cambridge bastard?" to one of the cows in the field.

Anyway on the way back once the shock of our relegation sank in we started to look forward to being a big fish in a little pond the following season as well as the prospect of coming up against our local rivals 'The Pigs' who were already loitering in the third division.

Chapter 4

PICKING UP PUNKS AND DUMPING A DRUNK

Bury 1 – 2 Blades
20th October 1979

Brentford 1 – 2 Blades
23rd October 1979

Swindon Town 3 - 2 Blades
3rd November 1979

Blades 0 – 2 Brentford
16th November 1979

Blades 3 – 0 Burscough
24th November 1979

Our first season in the Third Division started well and a run of eight wins in ten games put us at the top of the table and got our fans travelling in big numbers again.

We had already been away to Chester, Hull, Mansfield, Blackpool and Rotherham and had established ourselves as a top team sweeping away all that came before us with little difficulty. The problem was that the quality of the hooligan opposition was low and at most of the above games the home fans just did one at the first sight of us and meaningful scuffles were few and far between. I had spoken to Jimmy about joining us for some away trips and he said he would but had committed to going to some of the early games with another crew so we left it at that for the time being.

At the end of October we played away to Bury and we expected and got much of the same, no hooligan opposition, a 2-1 win and little to write home about. Except that two things happened at that game. One was that Benny started to get on my tits. He was always a heavy drinker but had started to become a liability by getting totally off his face before every game. At this match he broke all records and was shit faced before we had even arrived in Bury. He collapsed on the pavement as soon as he got out of the van and we had to drag him to the ground where he spent the entire match in a near coma. Just as well there was no real action to contend with.

The other thing that happened was that on the way home I stopped to pick up two hitch hikers on the slip road to the motorway who turned out to be fellow fans that had been left behind after the game. The hitch hikers were also punk rockers and female. I shoved Benny into the back of the van with the rest of the lads and one of the punks while the other punk bird sat in the front seat next to me. She was quite a sight, she had straight shoulder length hair parted down the centre, one half was bleached as near white as hair would go, the other half was bright red in a display of team colours taken to the extreme. She was quite a pretty girl once you looked beyond the bright hair and slashed clothing and something in her eyes told me that beyond the hard front there was more to her. Maybe it was an intelligence that suggested that, like me, she hankered for something beyond the cheap thrill but was quite happy taking the thrill while it was there.

34

As we headed home we talked and it soon became clear that these girls were up for the action at football. They told us how they had been involved in several recent scuffles with enough detail for us to believe that they had been there even if I was still a little sceptical about the degree of their involvement. Girls going toe to toe with Blackpool fans in the alley besides the ground did seem a bit much. But time would tell.

As usual we called at one or two pubs on the way home, (we had earlier decided this would be a one day event), and the girls started to show something of their pedigree, more than likely a show put on for our benefit, by getting us thrown out of each pub for unruly behaviour. By the end of the night I had seen enough to reckon that these two were as good as some of the lads who had been on one or two of our trips so I asked them if they fancied coming to Brentford with us for the match coming up on Tuesday night. They said yes and we arranged to meet on Tuesday in a pub down town.

On the Tuesday Benny and I picked up the girls as arranged and set off for London. As we had set off at one o clock and the match didn't kick off until seven thirty I decided to stop a couple of times on the way down. It was at the first stop I realised that these girls were going to be a right handful. While waiting in a queue for food at a motorway service station the girls appearance attracted one or two comments from a couple of lorry drivers sat nearby. Instead of just letting it ride (they must have had similar comments made all the time with their outrageous looks) Max, the one with the red and white hair, threw a plate of food at one of the lorry drivers and offered to fight him on the car park. Class chick!!

We somehow managed to get away from the services without getting nicked or set upon by a gang of angry truckers and stopped at two more services without further incident, other than finding out the girls were short on cash and would not have enough to pay to get into the match. I was not about to cop for paying for them so I said that we should be able to get in the ground for free by jumping the turnstiles, a trick we had done a few times before. Mandy the other punk girl said we were not to worry as they would be able to sort it when we got to the ground.

We arrived in London at about six o clock and managed to get parked on a dodgy looking council estate close to the ground. As it was a bit early for the match we wandered around and found a pub in the shadow of the Chiswick fly over where we managed to have a couple of quiet pints. As kick off time grew closer we decided to move nearer to the ground and as luck would have it there was a pub right next to the away end so we went inside for another drink. As was usual that season we had a good following and the pub was full of our fans with just a few Brentford fans keeping quiet in one corner.

We knew nothing of Brentford as a fighting force and were expecting little trouble and looked like getting none until, at about seven o clock, half a dozen handy looking lads in blue and white scarves entered the pub. They were a set of cheeky bastards all wearing their colours and walking bold as brass into a pub full of fans from two other teams. It didn't take long and before they had taken six steps into the pub one of our lads had confronted them.

"Who the fuck are you?" he asked.

"We're QPR." said one of them and grabbed our lad by the lapels of his coat. Seeing it was going to kick off I stuck the head on one of the cheeky bastards who was by now stood beside me and without hesitation Max swung her pint pot, the big chunky kind, and cracked one of the other Rangers fans on the head. He went down holding his head and the lad who had been grabbed put the boot in. The other QPR fans decided they were having none of it and did a runner chased by the two punk birds shouting at them and swinging their pint pots towards them. Like I said quality chicks! When the fuss had died down we looked to the matter of getting in the ground. The punks had said they had a plan and it turned out to be just like them, basic and in your face.

At the turnstiles for the away end there were large queues of our fans waiting to get in. The punks started at the front and worked their way to the back begging money claiming to have had all their cash stolen and not having enough to get in the ground or get back home. Quite a few people told them to fuck off but more people actually gave them something and by the time they had finished they had raised enough to pay for all four of us to get in the ground with some to spare which they split between us and while not making a profit on the day at least it turned it into a cheap trip.

Inside the ground was something of a non-event as far as action went, the fans were well segregated and no Brentford fans had come on our end. A few of our lot made a bit of a show on their end but were soon rounded up by the law and brought around the pitch to be put with the rest of us. We won the match 2-1 to make our record for the season so far Won 11, Drawn 1, Lost 3 and put us at the top of the league and odds on favourites for promotion. All was well with the world.

It was after the game that things went pear shaped. As we headed back to the van our mob was confronted by a good sized crew of Londoners. It looked as though one or two other crews had joined Brentford to come and have a go and it all kicked off on a corner just down from the ground. There was one hell of a battle but we never got close enough for any toe to toe stuff because of the size of the crowd. During the battle there were bricks, bottles and numerous other missiles flying around and at the end of it after we had had the cockneys on their toes there were one or two people in need of medical attention and the noise of the sirens from ambulances and police cars filled the air.

We made our way to the van and set off back home but were soon caught up in a large traffic jam. As we crawled back towards the motorway we saw the reason for the jam. The police had set up road blocks and were escorting any vehicle containing our fans away to wherever it was they took people. I decided I could do without being detained overnight so I managed to turn onto a side street and head back in the opposite direction. After a detour that found us heading towards first Reading and then Oxford we finally made it to the motorway near Northampton well behind schedule and well knackered. I decided to pull in at the next services and get my head down for a few hours. When I pulled off the motorway I was surprised to find the car park crawling with police cars and vans and at first thought something must have kicked off inside. Quite often travelling fans from different clubs would end up in the same services before or after a game and now and again this resulted in a set to. This time it was different.

I had parked up well away from the main building in a quieter corner of the car park so that we might get some rest without too much disturbance from other vehicles coming and going and we were about to go inside to use the toilets and grab a bite to eat when I saw one of our lads scurrying back across the car park. I asked him what had gone off and he told me that after the match they had found an old fellow dead on the pavement near the scene of the battle and were stopping all our fans and interviewing them to find out what had happened. Hence the road blocks in London. I figured it must have been a serious affair for them to have travelled this far from home to round up those that had avoided the road blocks. We had had nothing to do with this incident, being stuck at the back of the mob when it all kicked off and not getting anywhere near the action, nevertheless I didn't fancy being grilled by the cops who were looking for someone to blame so we all decided to give the services a miss and get our heads down.

Benny decided to kip in the back of the van with the two punks and from the look on his face I could see he fancied his chances of getting at least a feel of one if not both of them. While I found them interesting subjects I had standards and these fell well below them so I got laid out across the front seats which was by far the more comfortable berth anyway and tried to get some sleep.

The following morning we made our way home and I dropped the punks off and let Benny know that I would not be taking the punks along on any more trips. While they were up for the crack, they attracted too much attention plus they really didn't give a fuck and that attitude was soon going to result in more trouble than I needed. I also found out from the news that the old bloke at Brentford had dropped dead from a heart attack and had not been a victim of the violence and felt better for knowing that.

One other thing I got from this jolly was that I decided that Benny had not got long left on these trips as while there had been nothing specific he was just becoming more and more of a pain in the arse. I had also noticed that each time there had been an incident he had always been the one at the back keeping a safe distance yet when we were discussing events with anyone afterwards he always made out he was the main player. All talk no action I think it's called. For fucks sake even the punk birds had waded in and given it some while he stood on the side-lines.

The next trip was a week and a half later when we played Swindon Town. In between we had played Millwall at home. A few of the cheeky bastards had come on our kop but were seen off with little trouble apart from one big twat with an umbrella who tried stabbing a few of our lads with it before being hit from behind and disarmed.

After that game, which we somehow managed to lose, we decided that we would do Swindon as a long weekend and made arrangements to stop in Oxford on the Friday night. We didn't reckon Swindon would have too much happening but figured, with all those students, Oxford just might. So on the Friday night Benny, Malcolm and me were joined by a lad called Dick who I'd known for some time and who was the middle of three sons in a well rated family of stand firm hooligans and who I knew I could trust in a scrape. Dick was medium height about five foot seven and of a wiry build, he had short sandy coloured hair and could best be described as nondescript if you get my meaning. He had however a tendency to go over the top, never in a deliberate or purposely provocative way but it just seemed that it was either all or nothing for Dick. He would either sit all night without saying a word or swing from the rafters. You could never tell when one mood was about to change to the other so life with Dick in tow was always unpredictable. Anyway I was trying to find better quality crew members and thought it might be worth giving him a try. I had also asked Jimmy but he declined as he had already booked to go on a coach with a well rated crew. He did however say that after this match he had nothing else booked and would definitely come on the next one.

So on Friday night we set off for Oxford. We got into town about seven thirty after a bit of a scare on the way down when the ignition light on the van kept coming on. I cured it by sticking a bit of tape over it so that I couldn't see it! I parked on a multi storey car park and we wandered into the town centre looking for a decent pub. Nothing stood out so we went into a bar that was as near the centre of Oxford as we could find. The pub turned out to be a right dump. It was small, olde-worlde and full of middle aged snooty looking business types who looked down their noses at us as soon as we walked through the door. Dick bought a round of what was supposed to be beer but which came out of the pump fizzed for five seconds and then went as flat as a fart, and tasted not much better. We decided there and then that we weren't staying here long.

Malcolm decided to chat to the locals and I heard him ask a stuck up looking cow sat at the bar "Do you know where the biggest boozer in town is?"

The woman fell for it and said "No I don't."

To which Malcolm replied with his punch line "You're fucking looking at him love."

Malcolm stood laughing to himself, the woman moved to the other side of the pub and the rest of us just carried on drinking our flat ale, we'd heard it too often before.

Benny was getting restless so he asked the barmaid where all the young women went for a drink in Oxford.

"Try the Greyhound by the bus station, that's much more your type of place," she said, so the Greyhound it was.

As soon as we walked into the Greyhound we realised that we had been set up. There was no one in the place under twenty, no one over thirty and not a woman in sight. As we walked through the door and over to the bar a few of the customers shuffled over to the door behind us blocking any immediate retreat. We reached the bar and my first reaction was to pick up an empty glass with one hand and two sets of darts from a tankard on the bar with the other. Dick sensing what was going on did the same but instead of darts he found a pool cue in a rack on the wall at the side of the bar. Malcolm with typical subtlety picked up a barstool and turned to face the on-looking crowd who for all their implied threat and evil looks had not actually made a move towards us. Benny lacking any sort of intuition stood at the bar and ordered four pints of bitter.

"We don't serve scum in here," said the barman.

Benny quickly getting the message turned around to see the assembled mob around us, some of whom were now gently chanting "scum, scum, scum" getting gradually louder and louder with each chant.

"Scarper." I said to the rest and we bolted for the door through the crowd who by now were shouting "scum, scum, scum," at the top of their voices but who nevertheless parted and opened the door to let us out. Their only concession to violence being a kick up the arse delivered to Benny who was the last one out. Once on the street we could hear the roars of laughter from inside the pub and I had to restrain Malcolm who was threatening to throw the stool, which he still carried, through the pub window.

"Leave it," I said "they could have killed us in there, but they let us back off. Be grateful."

"We could have had them," said Benny.

"Yeah, well you go back in and have them if you want," Malcolm replied "I'm well out of it."

We did a couple of other pubs without incident and at closing time I decided to drive down to Swindon for a sleep rather than staying in Oxford. On the way back to the car park we spotted six of the lads from the Greyhound walking down the street and charged at them roaring as we ran. They heard the roar and spotted us in time to leg it down an alley and out of sight. No contact but I chalked it down as a moral victory as they didn't want to know about it when the numbers were more even.

I drove to Swindon through the night and the van was still playing up. I could not see the ignition light but knew it must still be glowing because the headlights were going dim and if I put the wipers on the headlights almost went out, so whenever the road was clear I kept turning out the lights and letting the battery charge for a while. A bit reckless but fuck it when you're young you tend not to think of the consequences of such actions.

Anyway we made it to Swindon and parked in a side street close to the football ground and got our heads down for what was about two hours sleep. I had recently added two inches of foam rubber to the back of the van and while it was not exactly luxurious it was far more comfortable than before. Along with an old continental quilt it made the night bearable.

The following morning we were out and about at six o clock, looking and feeling the worse for wear. As luck would have it we found a transport café not far from the van and we dived in for a greasy breakfast. We dragged our heels and made the breakfast last until seven thirty and then went for a wander around Swindon.

This was always the worst time on the weekend trips. The pubs didn't open until ten thirty, even the shops didn't open before nine so we wandered aimlessly for a couple of hours doing not much in particular. Once the shops were open we spent some time browsing in any shop that had some form of heating on to get rid of the early November chill and at ten fifteen we headed for the station to meet some more of the Barmy Army who were coming down by train.

This was the time when Persil were offering free train tickets in exchange for vouchers on soap powder boxes so hundreds of football fans were going through bins or begging boxes off their family so they could travel to the match for free. When the train arrived there were about fifty of our lads and we teamed up with them and did a crawl of the town centre pubs up until kick off time. As expected there was no opposition from Swindon fans but we had a good time drinking, dancing on tables and generally arsing about.

At two thirty we headed for the ground and while the main mob went on the away end we tried to get on the kop but were sussed out by the coppers so we ended up on the terrace as near as we could get to the Swindon end. Nothing much occurred other than a bit of banter with the Swindon fans on the terrace. These were not fighters, just ordinary fans so we chatted about football, life in a shit town (Swindon) and anything else that came to mind.

Half way through the second half Benny said he was going to see someone he knew who he had spotted further up the terrace and by the time the full time whistle went he had still not returned. The match ended in a 3-2 defeat and, as there was no sort of crew from Swindon to have a crack at, Malcolm, Dick and I made our way back to the van. With no sign of Benny ten minutes later I said "Fuck him" and set off for home. We later found out that he had been stranded in Swindon and as he had no Persil coupons he had to pay full whack for a train home late that night. As I said '*fuck him*'. As far as I was concerned we had got rid of the last deadwood in the crew and made way for Jimmy or any other decent thug that wanted to come along.

At the next home match which much to my annoyance we lost 2-0 to Brentford (who we had beaten 2-1 at their place not much more than 2 weeks earlier) I met up with Jimmy who said he would definitely be coming with us to Wimbledon which was the next weekender planned. He also asked if there was room for another one as he had met a lad at college who talked the talk and ought to be given a try. So I said why not and we left it at that.

Before that trip came around I picked up my second and last arrest. You wouldn't believe who it was against; Burscough. I know, you're asking who the fuck are Burscough and so were we. They were a non-league side from somewhere in scouse land and we had drawn them in the cup. As there was fuck all chance of any action on our kop we went on the away end more out of hope than anything else. Anyway as luck would have it some Liverpool fans had got thrown off the train in Sheffield on their way to fuck knows where and decided to come to our game. When we scored the first of our three goals one of the Liverpool fans smacked one of our lads round the back of his head so I waded in and planted one right on his forehead just as the cops rushed in to nick him. Seeing me get there first they decide to nick me instead, bang to rights or so it seemed; Bastards.

What they hadn't reckoned on was me having learned from my first experience and gone to court prepared to fight fire with fire. Having being daft enough to think that a simple denial would get me off at Hull, and suffering the consequences when I was accused of a load of shit I hadn't done and therefore wasn't in a position to defend, I went in this time thoroughly prepared and with a reliable 'witness' to testify to my misunderstood role in proceedings.

What I actually did was recruited the most innocent looking old bloke you have ever seen to turn up in his best suit and trilby hat and swear that what had happened was that I had seen the Liverpool fan start fighting and had moved towards him gesturing for him to stop fighting and calm down. He then went on to tell the court that he could understand that from the angle that the police were approaching they could have mistaken my arm movement for a punch but he had clearly seen my calming gestures.

The magistrates took it all in and not only apologised for me having being put to so much trouble but also said that if there were more people like me around there may be less trouble at football. What they didn't know was that the little old bloke was the father of three of the biggest criminals in my part of Sheffield and would have said anything I told him to for a few drinks in return.

The crown must have thought it was going to be an easy win because they allocated the case to a young female prosecutor with very little experience who I thought made a couple of vital mistakes. Firstly she never asked me why I was on the away end of the ground in the first place, bit of a clue there I think, and then during her questioning she made a bit of a dramatic speech aimed at painting a picture of me as a stereotype hooligan.

"I put it to you that you saw one of your fellow supporters being attacked by another fan and you were so incensed that you decided to take the law into your own hands and viciously attacked your rivals."

"I put it to you that you watch too much television," was my reply and I swear I saw one of the Magistrates smirk as she struggled to come up with a response. One-one I think.

While I still picked up a few ejections and the odd belting from the law I never got arrested again. Part of that was down to me being careful but most of it was down to luck because, as careful as you try to be, when the shit kicks off you have to get stuck in. You don't always get time to check your mirrors.

Chapter 5

BILLY KIP

Wimbledon 1 – 1 Blades
8th December 1979

This was a first for all of us. Wimbledon had not been in the football league very long and were still regarded as a bit of a joke around the country, although their results suggested they were anything but. Their attendances however were a joke and a motor bike and sidecar could get their away support to most northern grounds. So none of us had been before and none of us knew what to expect, except that it was London so whatever the standard of opposition at the match we knew there would be some serious competition around the town and so we would not be going in unprepared.

I met Jimmy and Dick at five thirty on the Friday, opening time at our local, the Devonshire Arms, which was a pub of two halves. In one side it was upmarket, a la carte eating, piped music and chitchat for the la-de-da locals who thought they were something special. In the other half it was anything goes with darts, pool and dancing on the tables to loud music from the juke box. We were needless to say in the juke box side.

While we were having our first drink we were joined by a tall skinny youth who walked in with a cocky bounce to his step and looked like a cross between John Cleese and Blakey out of '*On the busses*'. He was tall, about six foot one, and very thin with a pubescent moustache hovering over his top lip. He wore a pair of jeans that were torn and frayed around the knees and a T shirt with a huge collar that was a remnant from the early seventies and he walked with his shoulders pulled back, his arms slightly bent at the elbows and rotated his body above his hips as he took each step trying to make himself look broader. He actually looked like he was carrying two rolls of invisible carpet. He nodded to Jimmy and then walked over to the bar and said something to a girl waiting to be served who promptly slapped him across the face.

"Who's that knob head," I asked Jimmy.

"That's Stacey; he's coming with us."

"Stacey: That's a fucking girl's name."

"'Yep, his dad had a sense of humour."

"If my dad had a sense of humour like that I'd kill him."

"If he could find his dad he probably would, he uses it as a conversation piece now, thinks it makes him interesting."

"It makes him sound fucking stupid." I said.

Stacey came over from the bar with his pint and sat down with the rest of us and started talking. I wasn't really interested in what he was talking about but it seemed to revolve around how hard he was, how handsome he was, how interesting he was, him having a girls name and all, and how women found him irresistible, his opinion, obviously not shared by the girl at the bar. As he rattled on and on I thought about what a load of bollocks he was coming out with and wondered if he had ever thought about taking up talking bollocks for a living or maybe doing it as an amateur and entering the Olympics or something.

After about ten minutes of his constant drivel I could stand it no longer and interrupted him.

"Do you ever fucking shut up; not only have you got a fucking woman's name you fucking rattle like one as well."

"Well its funny you should mention it but I have been told about it before I've never noticed it myself but I suppose- -"

"SHUT UP!!!" came the simultaneous cry from three voices round the table before he could talk any more about how much he talked.

In the brief lull that followed we quickly gathered ourselves up and headed for the van. Once inside I set off for Wimbledon and Stacey set off talking. Wimbledon arrived before Stacey came up for breath. Despite numerous pleas for a break, Dick falling asleep, Jimmy stuffing his head in the bunch of cushions in the back of the van and me turning the music up full blast to drown the noise he just went on and on, oblivious to anything else around him. He was so thick skinned it was untrue, no threat or insult had any effect whatsoever and in the end I just blanked him out using the technique I had long practised on my girlfriends frequent moaning and somehow I made it to Wimbledon without committing murder. I wondered why Jimmy had brought him along and how long it would be before Dick flew off the handle and hit him with something heavy. Tonight however all Dick seemed to want to do was sleep.

The motorway had been pretty clear for a Friday and we made good time to the Wimbledon area arriving around nine thirty which just left the job of trying to find the Wimbledon ground. The tennis courts no problem, the dog track easy, but could we fuck find anyone who knew where the football ground was. No wonder the attendance is shit, no one in London knows the club exists. We eventually came across the ground by mistake after circling the dog track and pulling up at a pub for refreshments, the pub turned out to be attached to the stand on one side of the Plough Lane ground. The jokes about Wimbledon being a pub team didn't seem so funny anymore.

Having sussed that this was probably the home crews local (if they had a crew) I decided to be cautious and parked the van around the corner and we walked back round to the pub. Even though we had said we weren't going to underestimate the opposition we waltzed straight onto their home turf without a care in the world and could have copped for a right beating if they had been anything like a half decent bunch.

Fortunately the pub turned out to be full of silly old bags with blue and yellow hand knitted scarves, interspersed with the odd anorak called Melvin or Derek or some other such name for a dipstick, so we settled down for a couple of pints of Guinness and a chat about the plan for the weekend. That is except for Dick who after sleeping all the way down the M1 and through some of London's heaviest traffic had briefly woken up to walk to the pub and order a drink and was now fast asleep on a barstool with no visible means of support. He was giving one of the best nodding exhibitions I'd ever seen, everyone in the pub was looking on amazed as his head then his shoulders leaned further and further forward before suddenly straightening up with a jump and slowly going through the process again. I swear the landlord was taking bets on how many times he would nod before falling off the stool.

We had decided to spend the night where we were until the pub closed and then go and find something to eat before settling down for the night in the back of the van. Then tomorrow we would do some exploring round this part of South London before the match and do the west end on the Saturday night before going home as soon as I felt fit to drive on Sunday. Simple enough?

Nothing's ever simple though. After a couple of pints of Irelands finest we were just warming up. The pub had started to fill up just after we entered mainly due to the arrival of a gang of bikers, who, it seemed, used the pub as a base at the weekends. They were a friendly enough bunch who seemed more interested in talking about their bikes than worrying about the four strangers in the pub. Then the inevitable happened.

Dick who had been nodding for about fifteen minutes finally fell off his stool. Only he couldn't just fall off his stool like any normal bloke. No he had to do it Dick style, so as he fell forward he woke up mid fall and in his semi waken panic he suddenly tried to straighten his legs. This only succeeded in launching him into the air like a rocket only he wasn't heading for the moon, no that would be too simple. Instead of the moon Dick managed to land on top of a table occupied by half a dozen bikers. They were not best pleased at losing their drinks to a semi-conscious sputnik and so they shoved him across the barroom into a table full of Dereks. Now fully awake but not sure of how exactly he got where he was Dick squared up to the most docile looking Derek and planted him one on the nose. At this, two big fat women in scarves (remember them) got up and set about Dick with their handbags. Dick, who was never one to stand and take it, then tried to stick the nut on one of the fat birds and shouted at the top of his voice 'Come on then you soft southern bastards.'

Just in time Jimmy managed to grab him and drag him out of the door into the car park. I tried to pacify the crowd as Stacey, who had been in a particularly quiet mood since arriving, turned to the bewildered landlord and calmly said "Fucking young un's, you can't take 'em anywhere."

After watching Dick cause such mayhem in what was probably the friendliest away pub we had been in on all our travels I shepherded Stacey outside and suggested that we finish the night off somewhere else. Because we had talked about where we were parked and intended spending the night to various people in the pub I decided that it would be best if we moved the van somewhere else, so we all jumped in the van and I drove around looking for a suitable place to park up for the night. I eventually settled on the car park at Wimbledon Broadway station. Firstly because it was not overlooked by any houses, residents may be alarmed if they spotted a van full of youths parked outside their property all night. Secondly, and the main reason, being that I had spotted the mother of all burger stalls right outside the station and I was starving.

Having parked the van and woke up Dick, who by now we had all started calling Billy Kip, (playing on the words from The Jams '*Billy Hunt*' which was playing on the way down) we made our way to the stall and ordered the biggest burgers they had and stood eating them as we discussed what we were going to do next. Before we had chance to decide fate stepped in as it usually does.

Dick was standing staring into space as he munched on his burger and no one was saying much in particular when a car pulled up on the road about five yards from where we were stood. Looking into the car I could see it was occupied by three lads and a couple of girls about our own age. One of the lads got out of the car and walked over to Dick then taking hold of Dick's trouser leg he turned to the car and shouted to the occupants "Look he's wearing trousers, will he do?"

Dick wondering what the fuck was going on said "Oi what's the crack?"

The cockney bloke then turned his attention to Dick and said, "This is the fucking crack mate" and started swinging wild punches at Dick who, with some boxing experience behind him, bobbed and weaved around the punches while trying to work out how to twat this bloke without losing the rest of his burger.

The rest of us decided to join the action expecting the other lads in the car to join in but found instead that from out of nowhere we were surrounded by a dozen youths all spoiling for a fight, some armed with sticks. Judging this to be a well-practised set up I quickly said to Jimmy "Battle our way through and get down the tube."

Without hesitation Jimmy leapt at the youth swinging at Dick and, bringing his foot up to head height, kicked him in the ear. The crowd around us moved in intent on giving us a kicking. I was confronted by a youth wielding a big stick. As I backed off out of range another youth swung a long stick at Stacey who ducked allowing the stick to follow through and hit the youth who had been aiming his stick at me, causing him to drop his weapon on the ground. I immediately piled in and planted my best shot on his chin knocking him back and turned my attention to the other guy with a stick. As he squared up to me and took aim with his stick Stacey jumped on his back and gave him a sort of bear hug effectively pinning his arms to his side and rendering the stick useless. I, not being the sort to miss a chance, kicked him squarely in the bollocks and turned to see Jimmy holding back four more youths with the stick that my first attacker had dropped.

While we were outnumbered some of the mob were only young and inexperienced and were clearly only there to make up the numbers. Three or four of these youngsters had backed off in the face of this unexpected resistance and it looked as though we might be getting the best of this crew when suddenly we were startled by the approaching blue lights and sirens of a police car.

"Leg it." I shouted to the others and, as one, we turned and ran into the station as the police jumped out of the car and grabbed two of the nearest youths. As we reached the station platform, via a quick leap over the turnstile, a tube train was just about to leave so we jumped on board and sailed off leaving the law and the locals behind to fight amongst themselves. We jumped off the train at the next station, Jimmy figuring that there would not have been time to alert the transport police to pick us up yet but there may be if we stayed on for any distance. We therefore found ourselves about two hundred yards from the Wimbledon ground where we had started from earlier in the evening. There was no sign of any other pubs or clubs so we decided that we would slowly make our way back to the station car park and if the coast was clear we would call it a night.

We got back to the station car park and watched from the shadows as the police were packing some of the local youths into the back of a riot van. It turns out that rather than chase after us the locals had turned on the first police to arrive and after being joined by more of their mates a mini riot had ensued with reinforcements having to be summoned from the local nick to control the situation. Luckily the riot had not spread onto the car park and the van was intact so we got our heads down for the night and tried our best to get some sleep. We were only partly successful (except Dick who slept like a top) due to the cold and the smell of Jimmy's feet which pervaded the air despite us making him sleep with his feet out of the window for a while even though it was freezing and he could have got frostbite.

We woke early on the Saturday morning and having not had a skin full the previous evening felt pretty good, except for the usual stiffness associated with sleeping in a freezing cold tin box on wheels which we soon walked off. After a breakfast in a greasy spoon café we did a bit of sightseeing along Wimbledon Broadway and found a YMCA where we sneaked in and had a good wash and brush up. We then lounged about in a big communal hall until someone sussed that we weren't supposed to be there and threw us out.

Stacey then decided that he wanted his hair cut so we found a barber and watched as the barber gave him a quite good hair cut despite the constant commentary from Stacey throughout the process. After paying a fiver for the pleasure, Stacey left feeling at his neck and muttering about been seen to by a *'fucking butcher not a barber'*. We all wound him up by telling him it looked a right fuck up from behind until Stacey threatened to put a litter bin through the barber's window and we had to calm him down by assuring him that his hair looked the dog's bollocks.

All this activity passed the time nicely until the pubs opened and we went in to the first pub we could find and settled down to a steady Saturday dinner session involving darts, cards and a kip on the bench seating for Dick. I began to wonder if he'd been bitten by a tsetse fly with all this sleeping.

We had expected a few Wimbledon fans in before the match but I suppose that was being a bit optimistic so at half past two we set off on the mile or so walk to the ground. I couldn't believe it was a match day, even on the final approach to the ground there was only a scattering of people around and they were all our fans.

When we got to the ground we headed casually over to the turnstiles marked home supporters and went on to their kop. Once inside we found the kop to be populated by a few old men and some of the same sort of fat birds that had been in the pub the previous evening and it looked like we were in for a tedious afternoon. On the opposite side our lot had packed in behind the goal and were in a bit of a party mood as had become the norm at away matches lately. I

52

suggested we got ourselves moved over to the other end by the police. This was normally simply a case of declaring your allegiance to the coppers who would then swiftly escort you around the pitch to your own fans to avoid any trouble.

Jimmy went to the front and summoned a copper over telling him that we were away fans and wanted to go over to the other end. The copper just told him we would have to stay where we were as it was unlikely that there would be any bother with the home crowd who were in his words "The best behaved in the league."

Or in Dicks words "A right set of southern Nancy boy bastards with no bollocks."

This had the desired effect of getting us removed from the kop but rather to our dismay also saw us removed from the ground which wasn't quite what we had hoped for.

Finding ourselves outside again with minutes to kick off and a limited budget we wandered round the ground looking for somewhere that we could sneak in. To one side of the end where our supporters were stood we found one of the easiest illicit entrances to a football ground we had seen in years. The wall around the ground was made of concrete slabs and stood about eight feet high. Tight up against the wall was a concrete street sign supported by two posts about four feet high. On the other side of the wall inside the ground was a burger stall providing perfect cover for anyone jumping over. It might as well have had a sign saying '*free entry*'. It's just a pity we didn't see it before we paid to get in at the other end, the money we could have saved would have bought us a couple of extra pints that night.

Having climbed into the ground without any problems Jimmy, Stacey and myself stood and watched a reasonably entertaining game which ended up in a one all draw which was probably a fair result as we were a little below par on the day. Dick continued his sleep marathon by finding one of the few empty spaces on the terrace and lying down for 90 minutes kip disturbed only when we scored and some inconsiderate oaf jumped on him while celebrating.

After the game we set off for what was always the highlight of any away trip to the London area, a night in the west end. We got on the tube at the same station that we had got off when we had fled from the coppers the previous night and after changing at Earls Court emerged in Piccadilly Circus about twenty minutes later.

Sometimes there is action on the tube station platforms as fans from up to ten or twelve different clubs make their way around London after the game. This time the only incident of note was when a ticket collector at Piccadilly decided to try and stop fifty of our hooligans from jumping over the barriers as we hadn't paid for the ride. He was obviously new to the job as experienced collectors know that at half past five on a Saturday night the best way of avoiding a good kicking is to stay in the booth and pretend it isn't happening. At this time hundreds of crazed football fans stampede around the tube system like migrating wildebeest, hurdling barriers and fences and trampling anyone foolish enough to be blocking their path, particularly if they are wearing a uniform and daft hat.

As was usual when we played in London we made our way to the Cockney Pride and met up with more of our supporters and had a couple of pints before starting a six hour pub crawl around the Soho area. It usually took the same sort of form with a few scuffles a lot of free drinking and the group gradually slimming down from its starting peak to an eventual nine or ten by the end of the session. People dropped off in ones and twos, getting lost between pubs or in scuffles, getting arrested, pulling (very rarely) or just fucking off when they had had enough.

The free drinking bit was always easy in the west end, as it was always so busy. There were several rouses that worked and by the end of the night we had usually used them all. They ranged from the crafty picking up of a pint off the bar, as some snob ordered a large round and didn't even notice a pint go missing, to the plain filthy habit of pouring left over dregs into an empty glass. There was also the subtle befriending of some southern wimp and persuading him to buy a round or the blatant mugging of someone's pint with a threat or a menacing stare. Whichever way was employed it always resulted in a jolly good session on the cheap. Occasionally someone would kick up a fuss and then shit himself when he realised the scrounger he was confronting was one of fifty in the same room. Now and again someone would blagg the drink of one of a similar crew and all hell would let lose but it all made for good fun and livened up the evening.

On this particular evening the first incident occurred when Dick, who had miraculously managed to stay awake for over an hour, decided to take a less than subtle approach and slapped a bald bloke round the head and said "Give us your pint you bastard."

In normal circumstances this may have worked as the average west end drinker was usually waiting to go to see a film or a show and would let most things go for a quiet life. Any Londoners who may have seen the goings on would have got not getting involved down to a fine art and kept out of it. Unfortunately on this occasion Dick chose the exact same moment to make his move as the team of mobile bouncers that patrolled several pubs in the area walked in to the bar. One of them, seeing Dick's action, picked him clean up off the floor and slammed him into a pillar in the middle of the room. There was a split seconds pause as the rest of our crew took in what was happening, and recognised Dick as one of their own, before a hail of glasses chairs and ashtrays filled the air. The experienced ones among our crew recognised this as the time to get the fuck out of there as the protectors of law and order in this part of the world were no mugs. There was seldom more than two minutes between a scrap starting and the place being crawling with bouncers, coppers and more importantly the other less legitimate enforcers who had an interest in keeping the peace for the sake of their profits and keeping their shady businesses away from the laws attention. While we were up for it with the first two the other lot were in a different league. We also knew that the priority of all three parties was to quell the immediate action and get it off their doorstep. Consequently we had only to move two blocks up the road and no one was interested in us again. So we scuffled our way into the street and headed for another pub we had frequently used while things quietened down. What the fracas did mean was that our numbers had been effectively halved in much quicker time than we would normally expect. But at that stage there were still around thirty of us on the prowl.

We did another couple of bars without incident and a fellow fan named Spike did his getting run over by a taxi routine to scam a few quid. This one worked almost every time. Spike stepped off the pavement into the side of a reasonable slow moving taxi and rolled about in apparent agony on the floor. The taxi would usually, but not always, stop and the driver enquire as to the condition of the pole axed Spike. Then the crowd would move in baying for the driver's blood and Spike would come round declaring no serious injury but pointing out the damage to his '*new*' £30 leather jacket which had actually looked like a pile of shit long before the '*accident*'. The taxi driver faced with the prospect of a lynching or a police enquiry would then normally volunteer to pay for the damage, which Spike would reluctantly accept and bugger off to the nearest bar. It was amazing how many of the normally don't want to get involved bystanders would jump at the chance to have a go at the poor innocent taxi driver who they obviously saw as fair game.

As the night drew on we did the usual rounds of pubs, taking the occasional curious look at the odd dirty book shop and marvelling at the numerous strip joints which we approached but never entered because of the ridiculous entrance fees and bouncers built like brick shit houses. At one point Dick was propositioned by an old tart, and acting clever he asked what he could get for thirty bob (£1.50).He almost shit himself when she told him to come down an alley and she would see what she could do.

We eventually came across a part of the area which none of us could remember visiting before and noticing what was obviously a gay bar (there weren't that many about in those days). Someone suggested we go in and wind up a few '*puffs*' so in we went. Once inside we discovered that the bar was of a two-storey design. We headed for the upper level, the advantage of height and all that shit, and found that there was a gallery which overlooked the bar downstairs. Some bright spark then decided it would be fun to dribble drops of beer down onto the heads of the punters down below. All quite amusing to certain small minds but, as always, someone else joined in and raised the odds by tipping a full pint straight down the hole. Then, that not being enough, another pillock did the same but this time left the pint in its glass, which landed on the bar, shattered into a thousand beer soaked pieces and was the final straw. Although we had the advantage of height by being upstairs we did not have the advantage of a door out of the place. We were soon being set upon by twenty or thirty of the biggest meanest looking arse bandits I had ever seen.

Jimmy managed to repel the advancing mob using a fire extinguisher which was conveniently placed at the top of the stairs. The drenching from the water stopped the advancing mob of Village People look-a-likes in their tracks and bought us enough time to leg it back to more familiar territory.

As a result of our latest escapade we found ourselves down to six in number. There were the four of us who had come down in the van plus big John, a Nigerian standing six feet four and about the same across the shoulders and his mate Taffy a skinny lad who looked like an insurance salesman. This was mainly due to the fact that he was an insurance salesman. Taffy could scrap like a paratrooper and had no apparent regard for his own safety. The latter being reassuring when you were in a corner and had to bop your way out, but it could be a little disconcerting if he was trying to lead four of you into a fight with a fifty strong mob of Spurs fans.

Being reduced to what was generally accepted to be too small a number to try it on with anyone down the west end we decided we would make our way to the tube and our various ways home. Big John and Taffy had arranged to meet up with the rest of their crew at St Pancras at midnight to catch the mail train and we had to get back to the van at Wimbledon. So we headed back in the general direction of Leicester Square to get the tube. As we walked Taffy started singing some football chants which put us in good humour but also attracted the attention of a group of cockneys stood in the entrance to an amusement arcade about fifty yards down the road. The cockneys on hearing us, and seeing our numbers were an even match for theirs, wandered out of the arcade and lined up across the width of the road. As we approached we all noticed the smallest of them who was stood centrally and slightly ahead of the rest holding a magnum sized champagne bottle which he began banging against the floor in an attempt to smash it. I couldn't help giggling as, after four or five unsuccessful attempts, the bottle eventually shattered and left him holding just a tiny piece of the neck and, from the way he winced, probably cut his hand in the process.

While this bottle smashing exhibition was taking place Big John had carefully undone the belt holding up his jeans and withdrawn it from the loops around his waist and was now holding it by one end leaving the heavy brass buckle swinging free. The cockneys stood their ground as we approached to within six feet of them. Then before anyone had a chance to make any remark Big John swung the belt, the buckle crashing against the side of the head of the youth who had just smashed the bottle sending him falling onto the broken glass on the floor. Instantly the rest of us ran at our opposite numbers and laid in for what was only about fifteen seconds of hand to hand combat before the cockneys decided enough was enough and did a runner. We then headed down to the tube station and went our separate ways ending the night on a high, having enhanced our reputations among our contemporaries, and made our way back to the van for another restless night before heading back home early on Sunday morning.

I suppose it was on the way back from this match that I first really started questioning why I was bothering with this whole palaver. I mean I had a decent job and a hope for some sort of decent future involving kids, houses and holidays in the sun. But I was risking it all picking fights with low lives and dip shits and scrounging beer and scraps of food when I had over an hundred quid in my pocket.

I ran the events of the weekend over in my mind and wondered what I had been thinking about picking on queers when I held no grudge against them. The more puffs there are the less competition there is for the birds. That's how I'd always seen it. The other thing is while it's all well and good going back with the tales of how we'd triumphed over whoever it was, our luck would not hold forever and sooner or later we were going to come a cropper and either get arrested or badly injured. Either way the rosy future would be well compromised. I was no fool, I knew that I couldn't be jack the lad forever, you can't be a hooligan when you're drawing your pension can you? On the other hand while it was all happening I got such a buzz. So for the time being I put my thoughts to the back of my mind.

Chapter 6

CHRISTMAS CATASTROPHY

Pigs 4 -0 Blades
26th December 1979

The next away game following Wimbledon was on Boxing Day, part of a three game Christmas programme that was to be the turning point in our season as far as our football fortunes were concerned and a day our local opponents would harp on about for ever afterwards.

Christmas is always a funny time for football. There are usually three or four games crammed into a week, which can get very expensive. Also you are usually totally arseholed on all the booze and stuffed like a fat bastard on all the fucking turkey and mince pies, which doesn't help in a scrap. Then there are these fucking derbies, some twat at Lancaster Gate who can't be bothered to travel more than twenty miles to see a game had programmed the FA computer to throw up all the big local derbies at Christmas.

I don't like derbies; the build-up always gets out of hand. Sometimes you'd think it was the World Cup final people were talking about not a third division game between two average to poor teams from Sheffield. Then there's the aftermath, great if you've won, but lose and it's a fucking nightmare. For months afterwards every bastard that has ever been to watch your rivals (and plenty that haven't) gives you grief and takes the piss.

This one was the worst ever. We were playing them at Hillsborough. We were at the top of the table and everyone's favourites for promotion. They (The Pigs) were struggling in mid table and going nowhere. Bookmakers wouldn't take bets on us; even the Pig fans were expecting to lose. We lost four – nil and the bastards still harp on about it nearly forty years later even though we have beaten them many times since. Whenever they run out of things to say it comes out 'Boxing Day Massacre': For fucks sake move on!!

The game itself was something I want to forget; the dirty bastards kicked us off the park. They got our captain carried off injured and our star player was kicked up in the air every time he got the ball, to the point that he stopped wanting the ball; but hey that's football. The build-up involved many skirmishes down town in the weeks leading up to the game and there was talk of us having them on their kop. In the event apart from a minor set to when a few of our crew had a pop in the bottom corner there wasn't much trouble. Most people were just glad to get tickets and getting enough people on to their end to make a serious challenge just wasn't going to happen.

This was when the Pigs still had a fairly useful crew and we were only just getting recognised as major players. Things have changed in the years since and while our reputation grew theirs diminished at a similar rate. So in the build up to the match we were more interested in how many goals we were going to stick past them than whether we would turn them over on the terraces. Anyway from what I had seen of these encounters before, and opportunities had been limited in recent years due to us being in different divisions, the aggro never got far. When two large crews faced up there were usually too many people who knew each other well on opposing sides for it to get too rough. Friends, colleagues, even families had split allegiances and you had to live and work with these people away from football. There were actually far more encounters with The Pigs involving small crews on Friday nights down town than there ever were at the games.

After this game it was a different matter we were in the mood for a big showdown, our pride had been hurt and we wanted blood. We marched around their territory searching for a crew to take on but despite there having been a then record third division attendance we could not find any sort of mob that was up for it. They were probably too busy rolling about laughing at the ease at which they had beaten us to be bothered with fighting us.

We walked all the way back into town looking for them but apart from the odd couple of youths shouting obscenities from a safe distance they were nowhere to be found. As we approached the town centre we found a pub that was actually open, most having closed on police advice. The ones that did open on these occasions were either run by money grabbing landlords, who raised the price of the beer for the day, or by owners looking for a refit from the insurance money when things went tits up. On entering this particular bar I thought to myself that we were definitely in insurance claim territory. The carpets were threadbare, the furniture looked like junk shop rejects and the decorations were pre-war. We trooped into the bar and ordered drinks but the post-match atmosphere was the strangest I had known. The anger had gone from most of us and what we now had was forty odd hooligans in a pub slowly waking up to the fact that their team had been well and truly hammered. When we returned to work after Christmas we were going to get it rubbed in over and over again and we would have to roll over and take it.

After two or three pints it did improve a little but I couldn't say it got back to normal. There remained a feeling of frustration in the air, not only with the result but with the fact that we couldn't find any Pig fans to take it out on.

Then things changed; The Landlord, a thin weasel of a man who had been scurrying around ever since we had arrived, emptying ashtrays that were only half full and wiping up the slightest drop of spilled beer, seemed to be obsessed with keeping the place spotless even though it was a shit hole and he was getting more and more agitated with the crowd. I remember looking around at the place and noticing that while all the fixtures and fittings were well past their sell by date they were actually very clean and it was a lack of investment rather than a lack of effort that led to the scruffy feel of the place.

The landlord was doing his best to keep the place tidy but seemed to be fighting a losing battle. Others were picking up on the landlord's activities and starting to take the piss. One lad threw a rolled up chewing gum wrapper on the floor near to the landlords feet. The landlord bent down to pick it up at once, as he did with the two or three bits of litter that quickly followed. We now had ourselves a little game to play to take our minds off the days events and soon there was litter everywhere and the landlord, having dashed behind the bar to get a dustpan and brush, was now on his hands and knees sweeping furiously. As always happens on these occasions things escalated until they got totally out of hand and the landlord finally snapped.

"Stop it," he screamed "I try my best and this is what happens. You're all morons!"

That helped!! I've always found that there's nothing better than showing a gang of pissed off hooligans that they're getting to you, to really start them getting to you. The objects being thrown started getting bigger. Beer mats then a crisp packet were thrown and the landlord got more and more worked up as he tried to tidy up. Then someone blew up a balloon and released it. Everyone cheered as the by now demented landlord chased the balloon as it zigzagged around the room before landing on the gas fire and bursting into flames.

"Put it out." screamed the landlord, now close to tears. The crowd obliged and three full glasses of beer were thrown at the fire, extinguishing not only the burning balloon but the gas fire as well. Gas now started to fill the room but instead of turning off the fire or getting out of the place the crowd were now jumping on tables and chairs and cheering. The afternoon's anger and frustration were being vented on this poor sad landlord who just wanted to keep his shitty little pub tidy. Then some pissed up fool must have decided that he was cold because he stood on a table with a box of matches in his hand, struck one and threw it towards the gas fire, which was still merrily spewing gas out into the room. It was another slow motion moment as all eyes followed the path of the burning match through the air towards the gas fire. Suddenly from nowhere the landlord flew through the air and caught the match, like Gordon Banks at his peak, preventing an explosion but burning his hand in the process.

I decided enough was enough and slipped out of the door to make my way home just in time as I heard the sounds of sirens approaching the pub.

That night I watched Where Eagles Dare on the TV with my girlfriend and some of her family who were mostly Pig fans. I just sat there in a daze not seeing anything on the screen as I automatically nibbled on sausage rolls and mince pies until it was time to go home.....I hate Christmas!!

Chapter 7

LYING PAT AND A BLOODY FLAT

Exeter City 3 – 1 Blades
12th January 1980

January 1980. The first away match of any significance was Exeter City. Not a big name but far enough away to justify a weekender so it was arranged. Jimmy, Dick and Stacey were coming along but as this was a long trip we were looking for another passenger to help with the economics. Having phoned one or two lads up and not got any takers we decided to call at a pub in town frequented by a lot of our fans. We fell lucky as there were about twenty lads who were having a few pints before getting an overnight train to Exeter with their Persil coupons. Among them was a long haired, bearded geezer we knew from the home matches as Lying Pat (do I need to explain?) Pat told us that he had no coupons and could not afford the full train fare so I negotiated a fair price and he joined us in the van.

The journey to Exeter was interesting to say the least. Pat kept us entertained with the stories of where he had been, what he had done etc. etc. I calculated in my head that if he had done what he said, when he had said for as long as he said he must be over seventy years old! Anyway it passed a few hours and kept Stacey quiet as even he couldn't get a word in edgeways.

We arrived in Exeter about 2am so I parked near to the ground and we slept pretty well considering the cold and the cramped conditions. The following morning we woke early as usual and had a pint of milk each for breakfast after Dick had stalked a milk float, picking up pints from doorsteps as fast as the milkman could put them down. We then walked down to the station to meet the lads who were coming by train. After a bit of breakfast and the arrival of the train we made our way to the town centre where we met up with some more of the Barmy Army who had come down by coach. As the pubs were not yet open we found a football and had a game, about thirty a side, on the ornamental lawn of Exeter castle which was only ended when Dick booted the ball over the wall and down a steep hill towards Exeter Prison. While Dicks shot was not so good his timing was excellent as the end of the impromptu football match coincided with the opening of the pubs and so we all made our way into town and had a few pints as we did the rounds of Exeter's hostelries.

As expected we ran into no trouble and I used the time to make a few mental notes of the bars that might be worth visiting that night after the game. We had arrived too late and too tired to do the pubs on Friday night so we wanted to make the most of Saturday. One bar in particular looked promising; it was a downstairs bar under a row of shops. You could quite easily have missed the entrance trapped between two of the shops. A set of double doors, which could have been easily mistaken for service doors to the shops either side, sat beneath a small neon sign which was unlit in the daytime. We only recognised it as a bar because the doors swung open as we were walking past and the familiar sounds of the juke box and the clinking of glasses escaped into the street.

We went through the doors and down the wide stairway that we found inside. At the bottom of the stairs I was surprised at the size of the place as it opened out in front of us. It must have occupied the basement area of at least half a dozen of the good sized shops above and the well thought out artificial lighting along with the plush furnishings gave it a warm atmosphere. There were only a few locals inside but it had the feel of a place that would attract a lot of young birds in the evenings so it was marked up as a definite for a Saturday night visit. We stayed about an hour and found out the bar had a late license which made things even better and then we started moving towards the ground.

As there was no chance of any trouble arising we watched the match from the side terrace and chatted to a few of the locals. Then after a hugely disappointing game which ended in a three - one defeat our little crew went for something to eat at a Wimpy and sat talking over the teams changing fortunes while eating burgers.

Pat had met some lads he knew at the game and had said he would catch up with us at the van about six thirty. I asked the others and they agreed that the journey home would be better without a repeat of his fictional life story so we decided that we would move the van so he could not find us. I know that might seem cruel but he had so far only paid half the fare that we had agreed, and he was a bit of a twat!

We got back to the van and decided to drive down to the station car park as it would be easy to find if anyone got split up or too pissed. So after parking up we started to make our way back up into the town centre, pub by pub of course. In the second pub we visited we decided to have a game of darts and before long we were challenged to a match by some of the locals. Always up for a challenge we duly took them on and beat them in what turned out to be a pretty tight game. A rematch followed which we lost mainly through lack of interest and then they asked if we wanted a decider for a five pound per man bet. How could we resist, we all threw a pretty mean dart at the time and had turned out once or twice for the local pub while these Cornish pasties or whatever they were, were struggling on double two finishes.

The money went down on the table and with money at stake we all concentrated on our game and gave it to them proper. We won four nil with three of their team not even getting on a finish. Jimmy picked up the money and we were about to thank them for the company when one of them moved to the door and bolted it.

"We don't give our money to hustlers, give it back or it could turn nasty." he said.

I looked at Jimmy and he burst out laughing, here we were, four young northern hooligans being offered out by a bunch of pasty munching old blokes that couldn't even play darts and looked as though they would have had trouble handling a ladies darts team in a fight.

"Shall we give it to them?" I said to Dick

"Too fucking right." he replied and picked up an ashtray ready to launch at anyone who made a move. Everybody in the room, about ten people in all not counting us, backed off towards the bar and the bloke by the door unbolted it and said "Only kidding lads." Wanker!

Whether he was kidding or not the atmosphere was soured so we decided to move on, Stacey giving them some lip as we left.

We did another couple of pubs up in the town and then at about ten o clock we decided it was time to go to the basement bar we had found earlier in the day.

We knew something was wrong as we approached. There was a bit of a crowd outside and two coppers were questioning the bouncer on the door. We made our way towards the crowd to find out what had happened and were told some football fans had been in looking for trouble and had run into a large group of Navy lads that use the bar as their Saturday night local. The place was apparently a bit of a mess and would be closed for the rest of the night. We decided to get away before the cops sussed where we were from and we headed back towards the station where we found a chip shop and got something to eat. By the time we had finished it was after eleven so we decided to go back to the van and get our heads down. We had only had three or four hours sleep the previous night and were all knackered.

As we got to the van Jimmy said "At least we managed to get rid of that lying fucker who came down with us."

Stacey was agreeing when the van door opened from inside and Pat stuck his head out.

"Hi lads," he said "I've been looking all over for you, the van wasn't where you left it."

"No," I said "there was a bit of bother so we had to move it."

"That's ok;" he said "I found it on my way to the station and managed to unlock it with a lollypop stick."

I made a note to get the locks looked at, and not to park somewhere a stranded fan would obviously go, the next time I wanted to lose someone. Pat told us about the scrap in the basement bar which he had apparently been involved in but we all took it with a pinch of salt as it was Lying Pat that was telling the story. Nevertheless it sounded like a real good do, pity we missed it.

The next morning I set off for home early and drove without any incident until we reached the north side of Derby. I had the music on loud and almost didn't hear the siren as the police car approached from behind. The driver pulled alongside us on a dual carriageway and gestured for us to move over so I pulled into the edge of the road. After telling everyone to keep quiet I wound down my window and asked the cop what was wrong.

"You've got a flat rear tyre, I'm surprised you can't feel it." the cop said.

"Sorry mate, I didn't realise." I replied.

The copper had by now noticed the others in the back of the van and asked them all to get out. Instead of doing as I'd asked and keeping quiet some of them started giving the copper some lip. This is never a good idea and whatever options the copper was considering suddenly got narrowed down to giving us a hard time. My van got a thorough inspection and fortunately got through it, other than a couple of points where the copper wasn't sure if some of my accessories were legal or not. Because he wasn't sure he didn't push it. What he did do was demand all our names and addresses to check us out and because he had the van registration number I had no choice but to give him my real details. The others followed suit and he relayed all the names to the police station to be checked out. After about two minutes he got a call back on his radio to tell him that everyone checked out ok except for Pat who had a warrant out on him for non-payment of fines. The copper considered he had a result and took Pat away leaving us by the side of the road with one very flat tyre. What the copper didn't know, because it was the only part of the van he hadn't inspected, was that I had no spare tyre or jack on board. I had left them at home to save a bit of space. What a plonker! So there we were stuck on the outskirts of Derby on a cold Sunday morning, with only three wheels on the wagon, but at least we had finally got rid of Lying Pat.

We could see a few buildings just down the road so we set off walking and soon enough we came across a bloke walking his dog. I asked him if there was anywhere close that could fix a puncture and he said there were no tyre companies nearby but there was a car breakers yard about a quarter of a mile down the road. We got to the breakers yard and after a bit of negotiation managed to secure a wheel and tyre that had seen better days for a fiver. Unfortunately we were not so lucky with the jack.

Back at the van I decided that the only thing would be to try and flag down another car and borrow a jack. The others were getting restless and I told them to go for a wander as it would be easier to flag down a car on my own than with a gang of dodgy looking youths so they disappeared in the opposite direction from the car breakers yard.

After about twenty minutes and no luck in flagging down a car the lads came back. Dick was holding a jack and asked if that was what I needed. It turned out they had come across a caravan site and had rescued the jack from the back of a pick-up truck. I quickly changed the wheel before we were joined by a pack of angry Pikeys and set off for home. The delay caused by the puncture meant that we arrived home after closing time (2pm on Sundays in those days) so I went home and caught up with some sleep and rounded off another little away trip adventure.

Chapter 8

CHARLIE JOINS THE CREW

Oxford Utd 1 – 1 Blades
16th February 1980

February came and a trip to Oxford was on the horizon. After our encounter on the way to Swindon earlier in the season I was looking forward to going back and looking for a bit of payback. We had decided this was going to be another long one and arranged to meet On Friday in the Devonshire as usual. Jimmy, Stacey, Malcolm and I were confirmed and Jimmy had asked if a lad called Charlie could join us. I had heard of Charlie but had never actually met him. From what I had heard I was looking forward to seeing him in action. I was also surprised that he was coming with us, as he was supposedly a Pig fan. Jimmy explained that Charlie knew bugger all about football and didn't really have any particular strong club allegiance. He was coming along because he reckoned there would be more chance of action with us than with the Pigs and apparently action was his thing.

At 5.45 Charlie arrived and was not what I was expecting at all. At five foot five or six he was a bit on the short side. He had the sort of gypsy good looks that I'm told the girls swoon over and I wondered why he was wasting his time looking for trouble with a bunch of raggy arsed Yorkshire men when he could probably be shagging for England with his pick of the regions best totty. I found out in about fifteen seconds as Charlie approached the bar and called out "Give us a pint of fucking bitter love, I'm fucking parched, my fucking stomach thinks my fucking throat's been cut."

"There's no need for that sort of language" replied the somewhat bemused barmaid.

"Shut the fuck up moaning and pull the fucking beer." said Charlie.

The barmaid pulled the beer.

If I'd gone off like that I'd have been thrown out and barred but it turns out Charlie couldn't speak more than half a dozen words without swearing yet got away with it with no more than the odd look and a tut, tut, tut.

Charlie also had the most aggressive personality I'd ever come across. He even made thank you sound like a threat and his attitude must have frightened off most girls that he engaged in conversation, if he was capable of holding a conversation that is; which I doubted. He had a natural growl and a steely look in his eye that made people think twice before challenging him. A look I had been tipped off by

74

Jimmy that he couldn't always back up. Apparently while he could dish out the aggro he had been known to go down with the first punch that connected. More often than not this fact went unnoticed as most people bottled out before blows were thrown.

Charlie came over to us and sat down on the floor besides us even though there were plenty of seats available, there being no more than ten people in the place. We've got a right one here I thought but refrained from asking why he was sat on the floor as I was sure that was the whole point of his action.

"Give us a fucking fag," Charlie asked of no one in particular "I just smoked my fucking last one."

"You've always just smoked your last one." said Jimmy handing over a cigarette.

Jimmy had also tipped me off that Charlie was unemployed through choice and was consequently permanently skint and on the scrounge. I was surprised that he had bought his own beer.

"You don't fucking say much." Charlie said staring me in the eye.

"That's because I don't know if I like you yet." I said returning the stare.

"He told me you were a cautious bastard." said Charlie glancing at Jimmy.

"He told *me* you were a shit soft, pig, scrounging bastard." I said looking him straight in the eye.

"Looks like he was fucking right about both of us then," laughed Charlie offering his hand to shake which I took and gave a firm squeeze which was returned by Charlie who leant over towards my ear and added quietly "then again he might be fucking wrong."

"Maybe this weekend we'll both find out." I said.

Stacey, who had been at the bar, then came over to where we were sitting and gave a pint of bitter to Charlie without being asked. He then asked Charlie if he wanted a cigarette or something to eat. Charlie took up his offer on both counts and Stacey returned to the bar.

"Does he fucking fancy you or what?" I asked Charlie.

"No but he fancies my sister so he's trying to get well in and I'm making the fucking most of it." Charlie answered.

"You must be skint if you're prepared to put up with that tosspot," said Jimmy who had been getting a bit fed up of Stacey lately "they call him the growth you know, once he latches on to you, you have to have an operation to get rid of the bastard."

"I'll get fucking rid of him when the time's right." said Charlie smirking.

That'll be when his money runs out I thought but said nothing.

We set off for Oxford shortly afterwards and the trip was similar to the one to Wimbledon, Stacey talking, nobody listening and fairly light traffic all the way down. We arrived in Oxford around half past eight and after a quick spin around what bit of a city centre there is to Oxford, and pointing out the Greyhound where we had had our previous escapade, I found a pub on the road out towards the football ground and parked around the back.

Inside the pub it looked like a good place to start the evening. It was a big place with one large central room. It was roughly furnished and had a stage at one end rather like one of the working men's clubs back home. Off the main room were three smaller rooms one of which contained a bar billiards table and a dartboard, which is where Jimmy and I headed to get away from Stacey and his mouth. Stacey, Malcolm and Charlie sat at a table in the main room just to one side of the games room door with their backs to a wall so they could see what was happening in the rest of the room. We rarely had any trouble on the Friday night leg of our trips but after my last visit to Oxford it was best to be careful.

Usually we got on OK with the locals and so long as we behaved ourselves we were made welcome in most towns. We normally behaved ourselves on a Friday night because the main purpose of our trips was to see the football on a Saturday and we didn't want to miss the game because we were in some police cell or casualty department. The pub was a bit of a rockers place. There were several biker types about although I hadn't seen any bikes outside (motor bikes that is; you can't go anywhere in Oxford without falling over a heap of push bikes) and for the best part of an hour all we heard on the juke box was heavy metal music.

We knew the beer in this part of the world was crap so we were drinking bottled Guinness. To save us going back and forwards to the bar we had persuaded the barman to sell us a crate of the stuff which we had put under the table where Malcolm, Charlie and Stacey were sitting. We had split the cost and had decided that each person should stack his bottles as he emptied them so we could see everyone had drunk their share, or more to the point that Charlie had not drank someone else's share.

Jimmy and I had had enough of bar billiards and noticing that Stacey had decided to go and bore a group of locals decided it was safe to go and sit with the others while we finished the Guinness. Charlie got up and went over to Stacey to cadge a pound, which he then put in the juke box. Charlie then re-joined us at the table relaying the story of how the locals were taking the piss out of Stacey something rotten and how Stacey hadn't got a clue and was talking more and more gibberish.

We noticed that Charlie had already had more Guinness than his allocation but as he reckoned that Stacey wasn't going to shut his mouth long enough to drink his share we let it go. Then Frank Sinatra came on the juke box and the room went quiet.

"Your choice I presume." I said to Charlie

"Too fucking right," he said, "you can't beat a bit of old blue eyes."

The bottle counting system had been slightly fucked up earlier when someone had bumped into our table and knocked the empties over. We were now down to the last three bottles of Guinness and counting Stacey out, there were four people to share it. Much to Charlie's annoyance we decided between us that as we were sure he had already had more than the rest of us he could be the one to miss out.

Frank Sinatra finished and there was a sort of mumbled relief around the room. The next record came on and as Frank began to warble about Chicago being his kind of town the mumbles grew a little louder and more discontented and people started looking around the room to try and see which idiot had put it on. Charlie was still muttering to himself about not getting one of the last bottles of Guinness when Stacey came over and told us that the mean looking bunch of leather clad bikers over by the bar were talking about picking up the juke box and dropping it on the head of the next person to put Frank Sinatra on. A quick scan of the room told me that there were too many pseudo hells angels in there for us to tangle with and live so I said to Charlie "No more Frank Sinatra tonight mate."

"Bit of a bastard that," replied Charlie "My fucking Way's on next."

"In that case it's time to go." I said and the others agreed.

We got up and edged towards the door. All except Charlie that is who stood up with an empty bottle in his hand and shouted at the top of his voice "No fucking Guinness and now no fucking Frank," and crashed the bottle down on the edge of the table in an attempt to break it. Fortunately the bottle was stronger than the table, which was made of chipboard with a laminate top, and instead of shattering the bottle Charlie only succeeded in knocking a big lump out of the edge of the table. Nevertheless we had definitely outstayed our welcome. I dragged Charlie over to the door and as we made our exit the whole room fell momentarily silent. Then the juke box reverberated with the words "And now the end is near and so I face my final curtain…." followed by a crash as the juke box was hit by a flying chair which shut Frank up once and for all. I made a mental note that I should try that on Stacey to see if it would work on him.

Outside we decided to head into the centre of Oxford to see what it had to offer in the way of nightlife. We soon found ourselves in the midst of the ancient and grand stone buildings of Oxfords famous university, which take up most of the central part of the city. I was surprised to find that there seemed to be very little restriction to access around these buildings and decided we should have a look around, so we wandered up and down the narrow passages and through cobbled courtyards and I thought to myself that it all seemed like a different world to where we came from. After a while Charlie decided he had had enough exploring and said he was going to find a pub and wandered off down a passage heading back to the main road.

Stacey was rattling on about how if this was such a big university city then where were all the students, especially the female ones, who he reckoned would obviously all fall in love with him as soon as they laid eyes on him. I conjured up a mental picture of this skinny, thick as pig shit, mouth on a stick trying to hold an intelligent conversation with any female, let alone one who was studying who knows what at one of England's best educational establishments, and wondered whether the experience might just shut him up for good, but I doubted it.

Charlie was now out of sight and Jimmy said that we ought to go after him so we went back into the street. We could see Charlie about one hundred yards ahead. He appeared to be looking for somewhere to get a drink although if he found a pub he wasn't going to get far without Stacey's wallet. He would never have found a pub in this part of Oxford anyway because they all seemed to be tucked away down little alleys. Presumably this was so as not to spoil the architecture.

As we followed Charlie he was approached by a man who said something to him which we couldn't hear from the distance. We then stood amazed as we saw Charlie take the man by the lapels of his overcoat and butt him in the face. We ran the short distance to where Charlie was standing over the man who had collapsed in a heap.

"What the fucking hell did you do that for?" said Jimmy.

"I thought he was going to fucking hit me so I retaliated first." he replied

"What did he say to you?" I asked

"He asked me if I had a light." said Charlie.

"Have you ever thought he might just have wanted a light?" I asked.

"You can't be too sure with these fucking southerners." he said.

Suddenly there was a series of loud piercing noises from the man, who had produced a whistle from his pocket and was blowing it like mad. You know, like some demented copper in one of those old British black and white films where two hundred policemen would suddenly appear and chase a villain all over London. Whether that was his intention or not, we were not going to wait around to find out, so we did a runner into the town centre and popped inside the first pub we could find. We ended up in a downstairs pub come club with a live heavy metal band on stage in a room about twenty feet square. The place was packed with about seventy people listening to music pumping out of speakers the size of doors. The noise made waves on the contents of your stomach and would probably make your ears bleed if you listened for any length of time.

After closing time we headed back towards the van calling for a burger on the way. I didn't fancy the queue so waited outside the shop. As I was waiting I spotted a bloke walking towards me and went to ask him for the time. As I approached him he drew a big fuck off knife and said "Keep away I've got nothing for you."

"I only wanted to know the time you dipshit. Now put the knife away or I'll stick it up your arse" I replied.

I was taking a risk but I had found, in my experience, that if someone with a knife gives you a warning then he isn't going to use it unless he has absolutely no alternative. I took a step back and said "Fuck off and take your knife with you." which he promptly did. Funny place Oxford!

The lads came out of the burger shop and gave me a cheeseburger which I ate as my heart rate slowly returned to normal and I pondered on how we could go scuffling with gangs of fellow hooligans without seeing much in the way of weapons but could get threatened with a knife when asking for the time. It's a funny old world.

When we got back to the van, just to round off the evening we were greeted by the sight of four flat tyres, no wing mirrors and a bent aerial.

"Fucking brilliant," I said "well at least they've left the windows in."

I was fucking annoyed but there was nothing I could do about it there and then so we got inside and got as much sleep as we could in the conditions which weren't helped by the obnoxious smell radiating from Jimmy's feet. At one stage in the night we made Jimmy wind down the window and stick his feet out again but then we couldn't settle down because of the cold that was let in so in the end we had to let him bring his feet back in and suffered the stink.

In the morning I did a proper inspection of the damage to the van and was relieved to find that the tyres had been deflated through the valves rather than being slashed. I went to a garage and bought four tins of stuff in aerosol cans that can be used to re-inflate flat tyres.

This did the trick but wiped out my money for the match and the days drinking session. Jimmy, Malcolm and Stacey chipped in a few quid while Charlie pleaded poverty but the end result was that we had enough money between us to get home and have a couple of pints each at lunch time but nothing left to pay to get in the football ground.

"No fucking worries," said Charlie "I wasn't going to pay anyway; there isn't a ground in this fucking division that I can't get in for free."

So bolstered by Charlie's optimism we headed for the town. After meeting up with half a dozen of the lads who had come down by train and having a couple of pints we headed for the Greyhound where we were confronted by about twenty locals who must have wondered why a dozen youths had just wandered in and set about them without warning. After a brief skirmish involving a few overturned tables and a couple of well-aimed punches and kicks the Oxford lot did a runner and we headed for the football ground before the police turned up. No casualties but a bit of pride restored.

The Manor Ground at Oxford turned out to be a peculiar ground. At each end of the ground behind the goals there were turnstiles to get in, but at either side the terracing backed directly onto private housing with the only way onto the terracing being from the ends. We looked at the Oxford end but having not been here before decided it could be dodgy enough going on their kop anyway never mind doing a jump and trying to hide in a hostile crowd. At the away end things didn't look much better, inside directly behind each turnstile stood a policeman who was systematically searching everyone entering the ground so a jump over was out of the question. The wall at the away end backed onto an alley where our fans were queuing to get in and was about twenty feet high and too smooth and steep to climb. It was looking more and more like we weren't going to see the match when Charlie came over from the far end of the alley and told us he'd found a way in.

At one end of the wall where the away end meets the side terrace the wall dropped in height to about ten feet where it joined a wall belonging to the back garden of a house. The top of this garden wall was flat and about nine inches wide, there was another wall running

81

away from this wall at right angles which re-joined the football ground at the corner of the side terrace behind a hut, which we presumed was selling hot dogs or programmes. The trouble was that this second wall was topped with coils of barbed wire like something out of world war two.

"We can't get through that." said Malcolm looking at his new trousers that he had bought just before we had set off.

"Course we fucking can," said Charlie "I get through worse than that all the time when I'm nicking fucking lead off factory roofs."

So we decided that we would wait until just after kick off when everyone would be looking the other way and we would go for it. Jimmy was the first up, Charlie making a step with his hands and Jimmy using Charlie's shoulder as a second step to reach the top of the wall. I went second and then Malcolm joined us. It was Stacey's turn next but that's when the plan started to go wrong. As Stacey stepped onto Charlie's hand Charlie suddenly let go and dropped Stacey on the floor.

"You dirty Bastard." shouted Charlie swinging at Stacey and slapping him wildly round the head.

"What the fuck's up with you?" cried Stacey cowering from the blows.

"You've got fucking dog shit all over your fucking shoes you dirty bastard." shouted Charlie who was now kicking Stacey and wiping the offending dog shit in Stacey's hair. Jimmy, Malcolm and me left them to it and pissing ourselves laughing began the precarious walk through the barbed wire coils which although awkward was not as difficult as I had imagined. The barbed wire was fairly easy to flatten down as we picked our way through. Even so it took the three of us a good ten minutes to reach the back of the hut and another two or three minutes to check the coast was clear before jumping down behind the hut. Dusting ourselves off we found we had incurred the odd scratch or two and Jimmy had a slight tear in his jeans but we were otherwise unscathed. As we wandered from behind the hut onto the terracing we bumped straight into Charlie and Stacey who had found a much easier way in and had been laughing at us picking our way through the barbed wire.

It turned out that Charlie had chased Stacey, still calling him a dirty bastard, around the side of the ground where Stacey had ran up the side of a block of flats and vaulted a small wooden fence only to find himself inside the ground. Charlie had followed and, relieved at being inside, had forgotten about the dog shit. Stacey on the other hand, and anyone within ten feet of him, couldn't forget the dog shit because of the smell from his coat and his hair. We decided that we weren't putting up with that and sent him off to the toilet to clean up. While he was gone Oxford scored: Because we didn't jump about in celebration the Oxford fans around us realised we were away fans and because we were on the side terrace where all the non-hooligans go they backed away leaving us stood in a gaping hole. The local police spotted us and decided that we could not stand there, so they dragged us off the terrace and marched us around the edge of the pitch to the away end where we were unceremoniously dumped through a gate in the stalag 17 style fence and back among our own supporters.

We were stood by one of the corner flags and had a perfect view of anyone running up and down the wing but as soon as a ball was crossed the thick fence posts blocked out any view of what was going on in the middle. This ground must have had one of the worst views in the football league. The fence posts were so large and so numerous that the only way to see anything going on anywhere except directly in front of you was to either stand on tiptoe on one of the back two rows of terracing or to press your head up against the fence leaving grid marks on your face. We were too late to get the back row view and didn't fancy fence marked faces so we spent most of the match trying to guess what was happening from the reactions of those who *could* see.

I told Jimmy that I thought Stacey was a prat and that I reckoned we should leave him in Oxford but Jimmy persuaded me not to, mainly because he had sussed out that Stacey's mum and step dad had a caravan at Skegness which would make a great base for our planned end of season trip to Grimsby. Charlie was also keen to keep Stacey on board because he saw him as a meal ticket.

"This sister of yours must be a bit of all right for him to go to so much trouble to get well in with you." I said to Charlie.

83

"He's wasting his time though; she thinks he's a fucking prick." Was Charlies reply.

"Good judgement as well as worth one." I said

"Don't you fucking start," said Charlie "That's my sister we're talking about."

I wasn't about to get into a row about a girl I'd never met and who might have looked like a box of frogs for all I knew so I left it at that.

Stacey suddenly appeared at our sides, minus a coat and with his hair dripping wet and free of dog shit. I was beginning to see how he had become known as the growth, he had not seen us ejected and we could have been anywhere in the crowd, yet there he was back alongside us like he had never been away. I wondered how hard it would have been to lose him if we had decided to try.

The match ended in a one all draw and as we were low on funds we set off for home as soon as the match was over, stopping in a small town called Brackley for some chips with the last of our money. By this time I was getting fed up and all I wanted to do was get home, a feeling that I had started getting more often on recent trips. I don't know if it was the discomfort of the cramped conditions and lack of sleep or just that the novelty was wearing off but my enthusiasm for the long weekenders was definitely waning. The trouble was after a few days rest I'd forgotten about the down side and couldn't wait for the next one.

As we queued for the chips, along with about fifteen other fans that had stopped at the same place, and as the chip shop owner struggled to keep up with the orders I was beginning to wish we hadn't bothered. The wait for a bag of chips was getting a bit excessive. Suddenly the crowd in the chip shop started cheering. I looked out of the window to see what was happening and saw that our team bus had pulled up outside and the manager and first team coach were heading for the chip shop.

We were by this time about three from the front of the queue and not far from being served with our chips, which would have been the first food we would have eaten since the previous night's burger. I had not felt hungry before then but as we waited for the chips and the smell of the vinegar pervaded the air I realised just how hungry I was. The team coach came into the chip shop to be greeted by cheering and backslapping and then some fool at the front invited him to go to the head of the queue. There were groans from those further back as he ordered fish and chips twenty times for the whole bloody staff. Going on the performance of the chip shop owner so far I reckoned it could take him an hour to get round to serving us. I could be home in two so I beckoned the others to go back to the van so that we could get home this side of Sunday. As we got back in the van we could see the back of the team bus and spotted the team captain loading two crates of beer through the emergency exit. Fish and chips and beer while someone else drives them home, 'it's all right for some' I thought.

Back on the motorway I was just beginning to think what I might have to eat when I got home when the van started acting strange. I knew immediately what it was and pulled over to the hard shoulder to confirm that I had a flat rear tyre. So much for the claims on the can of stuff I'd used to re inflate the tyres in Oxford that morning. It was supposed to protect against future punctures. Now call me a stupid twat if you like but I had not got round to dealing with the puncture I had on the way back from Exeter and so we were stuck on the hard shoulder of the motorway, fuck knows where with a puncture and no spare wheel. What now?

As I was wondering what to do the rest of the lads got out of the van to stretch their legs and were wandering about nearby. I was stood just behind the van and Charlie, for no apparent reason, was laid on his back with his head under the rear wheel arch looking for who knows what. At that moment a car pulled up on the hard shoulder behind us. I could not believe it, it was a Vauxhall Viva, this car was carrying a spare wheel that would fit on my Bedford van and get us home. All I had to do was persuade the owner to lend us the wheel. The driver wound down his window and asked if we needed any help but before I could explain what was wrong, and do my best bit of begging to secure a spare wheel, Charlie pulled his head from under the back of the van, jumped up and in his most aggressive tone (which believe me is fucking aggressive) shouted "It's the fucking carburettor."

The driver of the Viva shit himself and, probably expecting to be mugged, screeched off in a northerly direction taking his spare wheel with him.

We were now back to square one and as there was more chance of winning the pools than anyone else stopping to help, let alone having a wheel that would fit my van, so we decided to try and find civilisation. We had stopped half a mile away from a motorway junction; I knew this as there was a fucking great sign that said A6, ½ a mile right next to the van. So we set off for the junction and whatever lay beyond. The trouble was what lay beyond was fuck all. There were no houses, no phones and no cars, so we kept walking.

Soon we found a side road with a sign pointing to a village called Lockington half a mile away, so we headed down the lane until we came across a house. Would you believe it, in the drive was a Hillman Imp. I knew that the stud patterns on a Hillman Imp were the same as on my Bedford van because I used to have a Hillman Imp (I know, sad twat) and had kept the alloy wheels which I planned to put on the van at some stage. So plan B, nice and simple, nick the spare wheel and have it back to the van. Plan B lasted thirty seconds.

Charlie approached the car (after I told him the engine was in the back and the spare wheel in the front) and lifted the bonnet. The alarm was loud enough to wake the dead. Who the fuck puts an alarm on a Hillman Imp? We all legged it into the darkness and after running for about five minutes found ourselves in another village called Hemington where we managed to find a pub. In the pub we spent the last of our money, which had been destined for the fish and chips, on a half of beer each and a phone call to my dad who reluctantly agreed to bring one of the alloy wheels out of the shed 50 miles down the motorway to get us out of the shit. Thanks Dad.

Back home the following day I spent what money I had tucked away on new mirrors and an aerial for the van and thought that if this was going to happen regularly then I was going to have to stop using my own vehicle. It was all right for the others they just chipped in towards the cost of the petrol and while I always added a bit on, it didn't even cover normal wear and tear never mind this sort of damage. There were only a few more away games before the end of the season and I decided that if I was going to carry on with this weekend lark next season I would have to look at using hired vans and hopefully make some money at it rather than it costing me a fortune every time.

Chapter 9

THE LIONS DEN

Millwall 1 -1 Blades
8th March 1980

Millwall came up in March. We had to go to Millwall as it was, at that time, the ultimate challenge. They were the big boys. All crews were judged against Millwall they were universally accepted as the benchmark for domestic hooligans. I'm sure Chelsea and West Ham fans may disagree but that's how we saw it. Millwall had been featured on the TV in a documentary that, while obviously over played and hyped up, was based on the fact that no one fucks with Millwall. We'd heard the stories, we'd seen the TV show and we'd been brought up on the legend. Now we figured it was time to go and see for ourselves. We were going to fuck with Millwall.

Millwall was not the place to go four up, so I made a few calls, looked up a couple of old mates and got me and Jimmy on the coach with the Barmy Army. These were the crew that had developed during our early weekend days. Like the crews of many other teams they started off similarly to us as small groups with no real line of command who just met up at football games and took what came. As a few of these small gangs joined up to travel to away games they developed into a highly motivated fighting force. Every decent club had their crew West Ham had the Inter City Crew, There were the Head Hunters of Chelsea, Man City had The Governors and according to the title of the TV documentary Millwall had three. F Troop, Treatment and The Half Way Line. New crews were cropping up all the time each getting more organised, all looking to get the headlines, and all originating from the efforts of the police to remove the fighting from the grounds. They hadn't succeeded in that yet but what they had done was to spread it out in to the community and through their heavy handedness and tougher sentencing by the courts had caused the need for the organisation of the thugs to avoid being caught. The subsequent escalation of the whole thing was fuelled by media sensationalism, to the point where outside forces were now being attracted to these gangs. Anarchists, political activists and even some pseudo para military nutter groups were all being drawn into what was developing into a war against authority rather than the reasonably harmless male ritual that it had started out as. It was this turn of events that was making me think about getting out as I had no gripe with the powers that be and I was certainly no political activist, I couldn't be arsed with all that shit.

Anyway back to the point, The Barmy Army had about seventy soldiers lined up for the trip to Millwall and were taking two coaches to London. The arrangements were that we would be arriving about half ten in the morning and picking up at Kings Cross at midnight. In between we would leave our calling cards in the Isle of Dogs and would come out with a heavy reputation or a fucking good kicking. One way or another we would get noticed.

The trip down was uneventful and there was no sign of anything out of the ordinary until the moment when we crossed the Thames. Then the atmosphere changed from one of a jovial day out to a sudden realisation that this was it. We were here. The Old Kent Road was no longer just a square on the Monopoly board it was a battlefield which if we were not on our toes could be the place we get our comeuppance.

The lads on the coach who up until then had been laughing and joking and lounging around sat up and focused on the surroundings. Streets that looked familiar to anyone who had followed hooligan related news, pubs remembered from the documentary, tower blocks familiar from programmes trying to blame the hooligan culture on social inadequacies. Here they were all around us and suddenly it was all very real.

The coach pulled up outside a pub about a mile from The Den and we stepped off with the adrenalin pumping and as the coach's pulled away we knew that this was it, no going back. One of the most respected of the crew took the lead and with no actual command being spoken the rest followed into the pub which contained about five locals who on seeing us enter, quietly got up and left without a word. We ordered drinks and took up positions around the barroom waiting for the attack from the Millwall crew which we expected within minutes but which never came.

After about an hour and a half and boosted by a few pints we decided that it was time to move on. We left and split into groups of about six or seven on either side of the road so as not to attract too much attention and with no sign of trouble made it to the next pub where there were about twenty five Millwall fans drinking inside. The first group to arrive went in through the main door while another two groups went around the side and found another entrance. This time there was a little resistance but after what was by any standards a minor scuffle the Millwall fans left the pub, but not with the usual panic you would expect in the circumstances. It was weird but they didn't seem bothered and a few of them walked calmly through a mob of twenty or so youths collecting kicks and punches for their troubles and yet there was little more than the odd defensive swing in return. It was almost as though we were being tolerated like someone tolerates a fly buzzing around because they can't be bothered to chase it about to squat it. The whole atmosphere seemed so unreal. After this we were again expecting an attack by Millwall so we drank and waited but the attack never came.

Kick off time was rapidly approaching, so we decided it was time to head for the ground. It was weird and again a little unreal but as we got to within a quarter of a mile of the ground it became obvious that there were no Millwall thugs anywhere. Sure there were a few older fans and a scattering of young kids in blue and white scarves but none of the hard core nutters that this of all teams were so famous for. Yet at the same time there was still this sense of menace pervading the atmosphere, almost as if our every move was being watched. We got to the famous Cold Blow Lane, what an appropriate name for this place, it was a shit hole; derelict wasteland, no birds, no animals just a few people walking towards the heap that was The Den and an almost eerie silence.

To reach the ground we had to pass under a railway bridge and it was as we got under the bridge that the first real attack came. As we began to walk under the bridge two whole paving slabs dropped from the far side of the bridge smashing to the ground just feet in front of the leading group causing them to freeze in their tracks. These things weigh about a hundredweight each and would have killed anyone hit by them, no question. Just as we were considering the possibilities there was a series of crashes from behind as another two or three slabs rained down from the other side effectively trapping our mob under the bridge for fear of being crushed by falling debris. These large missiles were then followed by a series of bricks, bottles and other objects being dropped from above, a bombardment that lasted for about one minute but seemed longer. At the end of this barrage there was a short silence for a few seconds before someone shouted "get 'em."

We charged out from under the bridge and looked for a way up to confront our attackers only to find there was no way onto the bridge above. We were again denied the opportunity to take on Millwall and wandered the last few yards to the ground with a sense of uneasy frustration. We had come here expecting trouble at every turn and prepared to get stuck in to whatever situation arose but we hadn't expected to be chasing ghosts. We knew they were there but we couldn't get to them and the odd ones we had come across just walked through us as though we weren't real.

At the turnstiles the theme continued, where you would have expected loads of coppers struggling to keep rival fans apart and hundreds of people milling around looking for confrontation all we saw was an old programme seller and a couple of youngsters who were trying to see through gaps in the fence. There was litter blowing around in the breeze making it seem like one of those ghost towns in a cowboy film. While there was now some sound from inside the ground it was not the normal sort of sound you would expect at a football match it was more of a low mumbling sound, a menacing growl rather than an all-out roar. Then someone had a brain wave.

"If they won't come to us let's go to them" he said.

Some other fool agreed and within seconds everyone was clamouring for a place on the Millwall end. I wondered what the fuck we were doing, but, caught up in the moment, I joined Jimmy and several others who were scaling an exit gate to jump into the Millwall kop. Some of the others took the more conventional route and paid to get through the turnstiles.

Once inside the ground the mystery of where the Millwall fans were was solved. Within seconds of entering the ground we were confronted by a small mob of the bastards who waded in with no preliminaries and had us pinned in a corner behind their kop and out of sight of any police that might have been in the ground. I was by now beginning to wonder if any police had bothered to turn up.

Not wanting to get a kicking in a forgotten corner of south east London we ran at the Millwall fans swinging and kicking along with the rest of our crew which was about twenty strong, the rest having not made it into the ground before the aggro started and were probably glad of it. The fight lasted no more than a minute, each crew giving as good as it got, the adrenaline pumping and while we were all picking up bumps and bruises no one was getting really hurt. For those couple of minutes it was just like when I first started the hooligan thing and so was the buzz. Things don't last though and with a swift change of emphasis the Millwall fans backed off in what we were about to find out was a well laid plan.

There had up until then been around twenty to thirty of them and although we were slightly outnumbered it wasn't a massive handicap. In the confines of the area behind the kop they found it hard for them to all get at us at once, the majority of the fighting was one on one and we were all experienced scrappers who could usually hold our own in that kind of situation. Now however we were about to be led into the lion's den (both figuratively and literally). The Millwall fans backed off and assembled at the end of an entrance to the terracing which formed their kop and beckoned at us to come and have another go which was like a red rag to a bull and so we charged at them. This was a bit of a daft move, as we had no idea what was waiting for us inside. The normal routine of surveying the scene and planning the best way to surprise the opposition had gone out of the window, so onto the Millwall kop we charged.

It must have looked good from the distance as our crew came running onto the most feared territory in football at that time, shouting and bawling, swinging at any Millwall fan in range. For about five seconds we were THE crew. Then we realised our folly, this was Millwall and if we were on their kop it was because that was where they wanted us. It was another of those time stands still moments as, before the storm, I glanced around and took in the situation like I was looking at a photograph or a plan of a battle field.

By now we were stood near the bottom of the Millwall kop, above us and to one side on the terracing were hundreds of angry Millwall fans. Some were wearing hoods with holes in for their eyes, many carrying makeshift weapons. Below us and to the other side preventing a swift exit onto the pitch or into other sections of the ground was an eight-foot high fence. Beyond the side fence was an area about ten yards wide, a sort of no man's land. On the other side

94

of this no man's land was a similar fence but this one had a chain link fence above it stretching all the way to the roof line preventing missiles hitting the away fans caged inside, in this case our fans. This was where we should have been, not out in the open squaring up to the bunch of savages now bearing down on us. To make matters worse it seemed that every copper in the ground was in the section containing the away fans forming a sort of human barricade between the two factions.

The mob of Millwall fans descended on us and pinned us into the bottom corner of the kop punching and kicking at the ones at the front of the crew. The rest were getting crushed against the fencing. At the very bottom of the fence there was a gate and in the melee someone actually managed to find the bolt securing it and pull it free which allowed us to spill into the area of no man's land between the two rival sets of fans. A few Millwall fans managed to get through but they were swiftly beaten back as we were now aided by the fact that they were all trying to squeeze through a three foot wide gap in the fence and we could pick them off as they tried to get through. Six or seven coppers eventually decided that it was reasonably safe for them to enter the fray and they swiftly closed the gate and under a barrage of missiles from the Millwall fans we were shepherded into the cage that formed the away end.

Once inside this caged corner of the ground we soon found that there was a flaw in the defences. We were bombarded with coins which were small enough to get through the fencing but heavy enough to do damage to any head they struck and several people found they needed medical attention to head wounds. This attack fortunately didn't last too long as it was a very expensive way to attack your rivals and even the more affluent southern fans had limits in what they could afford to throw. It had the bonus however of littering our section of the ground with quite a few pounds. I had no qualms about joining the many other fans that were picking up the coins, initially to throw back but then, realising the value, pocketing the proceeds as a kind of an unofficial compensation fund. I personally ended up with about ten pounds, which went nicely towards covering some of my costs.

The game went much as usual and ended up in a one all draw. Millwall got a late equaliser when a giant of a substitute came on and proceeded to knock the shit out of any of our players who got in the way before sticking the ball into the net. I swear to this day that he was not a player but some thug off the terraces who barged his way into the dressing room and demanded a game.

During the game there had been no more violence but the atmosphere of menace grew gradually and occasionally a hooded fan would throw himself at the dividing fence shouting and screaming abuse threatening what was to come after the game, most of which everyone now believed was going to happen.

At the end of the game the home fans left quietly and everything fell silent as we waited for the police to decide it was safe to let us out. At most grounds this was usually ten to fifteen minutes but here it was half an hour before the first movement. There was a tannoy announcement asking fans whose coaches were parked outside to assemble at the front of the terracing so they could be escorted to their transport. About three hundred and fifty fans duly obliged and were led away by an equal amount of police to the awaiting buses.

There was only a fairly small following of our fans at this game, probably down to the reputation of Millwall. There were now around two hundred away fans left inside and the police proceeded to ask how each fan intended getting home. We were soon sorted into two groups, those who had gone by private cars or vans and the seventy of us who were meeting up with the coach at Kings Cross later and intended taking the tube to get there. The police were not at all happy and after escorting those who were driving home back to their cars they held us in the ground until six-o clock. It was nearly an hour and a half after the final whistle before the police radioed their superiors to find out what to do.

Eventually it was declared safe for us to be escorted to the tube station and the seventy of us were shepherded through the gloomy streets of south east London. Around two hundred coppers surrounded us and halted us at every corner while someone was sent ahead to radio back when the coast was clear. I thought this was over the top but changed my mind when we got to within a hundred yards of the tube station to be greeted by over a hundred Millwall fans shouting for our blood.

The police split into two groups, one surrounding us and preventing anyone leaving the area and the other group charging, truncheons drawn, at the Millwall fans dispersing the crowd and clearing the way for us to enter the station. Once inside the police left us to get the train while they formed a human barricade across the station entrance preventing any returning Millwall fans from getting in.

We made our way to the platform having paid the minimum fare and got on to the awaiting train that stood with its doors open for what seemed like an eternity. Someone eventually asked what the delay was and was told that the train was not due to leave for another ten minutes as there had been some trouble at the next stop where there were some Millwall fans waiting to ambush the train.

As we waited another train pulled in to the station and two youths got off and wandered up and down the platform looking around. They walked past our train, which still stood with its doors open, and looked in as they passed, obviously weighing up the situation. We didn't pay too much attention, as it was unlikely that just two of them were going to have a go at seventy of us, but this was Millwall and the unlikely happens here all the time.

The two of them had passed our part of the train and it looked like there was no danger of anything untoward happening when suddenly one of them came charging at the train. He picked up a dustbin off the platform and smashed it through the train window where some of our lads were sitting, showering them in glass. They both then jumped on the train punching at anyone within reach.

Unfortunately for them they had jumped on the train right where the biggest bunch of nutters in our crew were sat. One of them pulled out a cut throat razor from his pocket and slashed it down the chest of one of the attackers who froze for a second before beginning to bleed profusely from his wound. Both Millwall fans then jumped off the train and ran up the stairs towards the station exit.

We thought that would be the end of it and sat bewildered by the nerve of these two idiots, but two minutes later, just as everyone was getting their breath back, we were startled by the sound of two more dustbins being thrown down the stairs. The two Millwall fans, one soaked in blood, then came rushing back onto the platform chased by several coppers. Then rather than attempting to make a getaway they jumped back onto our train and started fighting again. The police followed them onto the train and swiftly broke up the fighting and once they had calmed things down they asked the wounded Millwall fan how he had got his injuries. He told them he had been stabbed by a fan with a red star tattooed on his neck. The police walked up and down the train searching for a fan with a star tattooed on his neck and to their dismay they found five, all part of the same gang whose mark was the red star. As the Millwall fan couldn't identify the actual culprit from the five tattooed thugs the police decided the best thing was to get us off their patch as quickly as possible. The police took the Millwall fan away for treatment and let the train go on its way which was a relief to me and several other members of our crew. I remember saying to myself at that moment '*that's it, no more of this lark*' and immediately thinking '*yes, until next time.*' That's how it had always been, one part of me wanting out the other craving for more and I wondered just what it would take to get me out of it altogether.

That night we had decided to do Charring Cross rather than Soho, not a million miles apart but quite different in atmosphere. Charring Cross was still touristy but not as harsh and in your face as Soho and in many of the pubs you could actually sit down and have a fairly quiet drink. Quiet that is until some cockney git took offence at one of our lads jumping the queue at the bar and took further offence at the pint of beer he got poured over his head for objecting.

Casper (the one who pushed in) invited the cockney and a couple of his mates into the toilets to settle their differences. The cockney and his mates took up the offer seeing Casper as a five foot four northern fool and not asking themselves why this short, seemingly physically weak character had the nerve to challenge them on their own turf. They followed Casper into the toilets where he proceeded to show them why.

I forgot to mention that Casper was a total nutter who was rumoured to have been thrown out of his last two martial arts schools for being too aggressive, but not before collecting several belts of various colours. We all sat quietly while the group went into the toilets, listened to the short series of bumps and bangs and then clapped politely as Casper re-appeared and, holding his hands together prayer like, took a bow. The Cockneys did not re-appear.

We moved on to another pub where one of the lads read out the days football results to all the pub receiving cheers or boos depending on the way the games had gone and our feelings towards the teams involved. The biggest boos coming when he announced that the Pigs had beaten Wimbledon 3-1. The bastards were now looking like promotion candidates while our challenge had faltered and just about died. How shit is that.

The rest of the night went without much incident and as the drink flowed the atmosphere lightened and we ended up having a bit of a singing battle with some pearly kings and queens in a typical Cockney boozer. Our '*Ilkley Moor Bar T'ats*' going head to head with their '*Knees up Mother Browns*' with some football versions of their more traditional songs thrown in for good measure. It seemed crazy that lads who had been battling with the best earlier in the day were now having a sing song round a piano with some silly old fuckers covered in buttons and getting similar sort of kicks from both.

By midnight and back on the coach we had all relaxed a bit and the days adrenalin had worn off to be replaced by a tiredness that resulted in most people sleeping all the way back home. A quiet end to a crazy day.

Chapter 10

THE GOATS AND THE GLUE

Grimsby Town 4 – 0 Blades
3rd May 1980

The season had taken a turn for the worse and it was now obvious that promotion was not going to happen. This had dampened our enthusiasm a little and we went to the next few away games just as straight there and back runs, having decided that we would make the last match of the season something special.

We were to play the last match away to Grimsby at Blundell Park, a crappy little ground tucked away next to the railway lines where Grimsby becomes Cleethorpes. While the prospect of spending much time in either Grimsby or Cleethorpes wasn't all that exciting, Skegness, which was just down the coast, had a lot more appeal.

I had by now swapped my van for a car. Persuaded partly by my girlfriends nagging about having a more conventional vehicle, and partly because I was getting fed up of the discomfort of cold nights cramped up with three or four smelly drunken blokes in some strange town far from home. I thought that if there was not the facility to rough it I might persuade the others to part with some money and pay for comfortable lodgings on our travels. The idea was accepted in principle by Jimmy but Malcolm was a bit put out and Stacey said he didn't fancy having to pay for B&B for two every time. Charlie called him a tight bastard but Stacey was adamant on that one. It appeared that the lengths to which Stacey was prepared to go to get off with Charlie's sister had reached their limits.

Charlie had been working on Stacey and had eventually got him to agree to ask his mother if he could use the caravan at Skegness for a couple of nights and he had told Charlie that it was sorted. The government had also helped out by declaring May Day as a bank holiday so we made plans to go down on Friday night and stay right through until Monday afternoon.

Friday night became very late Friday night when my girlfriend reminded me that it was her birthday and she wanted taking out, so I arranged to meet the others outside the Claymore at eleven o clock and it was eleven thirty by the time we had decided that we had waited long enough for Malcolm who hadn't shown up.

By the time Jimmy, Charlie, Stacey and I arrived at Skegness it was throwing out time at the clubs so we decided to go straight to the caravan. Straight being an hour's tour around hundreds of identical looking sites because Stacey had only ever been twice before, both times being in daylight and sober. Eventually, more by luck than judgement we stumbled across the site. Stacey recognising a phone box by a chip shop which I reckoned we had passed at least twice before.

As we pulled onto the site and up to the caravan that Stacey pointed out, we received the first setback to our plans. Stacey yelled out "The fucking bastard."

"What's up?" Asked Jimmy.

"That bastard step father of mine; that's his car," said Stacey pointing to a Ford Cortina parked by the side of the caravan. "He's come to the caravan just to stop me using it."

"I thought you said *we* could have the fucking caravan." said Charlie.

"My mother said we could. That bastard must have found out and come here just to ruin it for me." said Stacey who was well pissed off by now.

It turns out Stacey and his step father have this hate - hate relationship and both go out of their way to make things awkward for each other, this being the latest example. This time though Stacey had had enough, he had been let down in front of his mates and he wanted to show us he wouldn't just take it.

Stacey got out of the car and headed for the caravan. He started hammering on the caravan door shouting "Come out you fat bastard, come and have a go."

The lights came on in the caravan and as Stacey continued to shout and bang we could see shadows scrambling around inside. Stacey by now was getting really worked up and was jumping around screaming. I had to stifle a laugh as the thought crossed my mind that he both looked and sounded like Phil Daniels character in the film Quadraphenia when he got his scooter run over by a postman's van.

After about a minute the caravan door flew open knocking Stacey backwards into the wooden rails of the decking that ran down one side of the caravan.

"What the fucking hell is going on?" came the question from a big fat bloke in a string vest and a pair of scruffy looking baggy denim jeans that he was still trying to get fastened up. He looked like

103

Oliver Reed on a bad day and as he spotted Stacey he bellowed "O it's you is it? You scrawny little bastard. What do you want?"

"You knew I wanted to use the caravan. You came here just to spoil it." wailed Stacey starting to sound a bit pathetic now.

"That's just the point," said step father "I didn't know did I. You creep round your mother but it's me who pays for this place and it's me who says who can use it not her and I say I'm using it so fuck off home and take your fucking tosser mates with you."

He then pushed Stacey knocking him off the steps and onto his back on the grass beside the caravan.

"That's enough." I said to Jimmy as I jumped out of the car. Up until now it had been a family squabble which I wanted nothing to do with but now this fat ugly lump of a man was going too far. He was obviously a bully who thrived on picking on the weak, and one thing I couldn't stand was a bully. I didn't mind equally matched pairs having a good scrap, be it individuals or gangs. I preferred to go in slightly outnumbered myself as it was the beating of the odds, the higher risk, that gave me the buzz but this bloke was just a wanker bully and it looked as though this was not the first time he had knocked Stacey about.

Jimmy and Charlie followed me towards the caravan and while they picked Stacey up I said to Stacey's step dad "Who are you calling tossers you knob head."

"Who the fuck are you?" he asked.

"I'm your worst nightmare." I said remembering a line I had heard in a film or TV show somewhere.

As I spoke Jimmy and Charlie stepped out of the shadows into the pool of light surrounding the caravan. It did the trick because as soon as he saw he was well outnumbered Stacey's step dad backed off.

"Bugger off or I'll call the police." he said.

"Call the police," I said "I'm sure they'll be interested in your assault on Stacey."

"He provoked me." he replied puffing up his chest in bravado.

"That's not what we saw," I said, "He's just come to see his mum."

"O fuck off," said Stacey's Step dad "and I'll see you when you get home." he said staring at Stacey.

"And we'll fucking see you if you touch him." said Charlie deciding to join the debate.

"Bollocks" came the reply as step dad retreated into the caravan.

I wondered where mummy Stacey had been during all this palaver but presumed she was keeping her head down to avoid being the next on step dads thumping list. I was sure she must have felt the back of his hand before.

We all went back to the car and I decided to move it just in case Stacey's step dad did decide to phone the police and we ended up parked on another caravan site about half a mile away. "That's the caravan idea down the toilet then," said Jimmy "it looks like it's the back of the car tonight."

So sleep in the car it was.

We were woken by the sound of the car door opening and closing. I braced myself expecting a raid by the local police but Jimmy, who must have been thinking much along the same lines, relived my fears.

"It's OK, it's only Charlie." he said.

"What's he up to at this time in the morning?" I asked having glanced at my watch to see it was six thirty a.m.

"He's hunting." said Jimmy.

Curious, we all watched as Charlie crept up on a milk float like it was some prized big game on a safari. While the milk man left his float to deliver milk to the site shop, Charlie nipped across to the float and swiped a couple of bottles dashing back and depositing his 'prey' under a nearby caravan. After three successful raids he waited for the milkman to drive off and then collected all the bottles from their hiding place and returned to the car.

"Milk or fucking orange juice?" he asked with a grin and passed the bottles through the open car windows.

"Brilliant," said Stacey "now go and stalk a butcher and a baker and we can all have a bacon sandwich."

"Can't promise that," Said Charlie "but there're loads of fucking rabbits out there; I'll catch one of them little bastards if you like."

"No thanks Charlie, it's not quite the same." said Jimmy. After drinking the milk and orange juice between us we decided we would have an early start for Grimsby so Charlie jumped into the car and headed up the coast.

We arrived in Grimsby just after eight in the morning and having parked the car reasonably close to the football ground, ready for a speedy return to Skegness after the game, we walked down towards the town centre. Charlie then decided that he had to find some toilets so he could get cleaned up. I had noticed during the time that I had known Charlie that he was obsessed with washing his hands. Although his clothes were tatty they were usually clean and he seemed to wash his hands at least once every hour. While the rest of us would usually freshen up after a night's sleep if and when we came across somewhere convenient, Charlie would not settle until he had searched out a wash and brush up and had a good scrub.

We found a public toilet near the town centre and wandered in. It was an underground affair with a flight of tiled steps going down and a brass handrail on one side. As we descended the stairs a man was coming out of the toilets using the handrail to help himself up the stairs.

"Have you washed your hands?" Charlie said to the man out of the blue.

"No as a matter of fact I haven't." replied the man somewhat taken aback.

"Well don't touch the fucking handrail then you dirty bastard," said Charlie dragging the man away. "Have you never heard of fucking hygiene."

As the man scurried up the stairs and away down the street Stacey said to Charlie,

"Was that called for?"

"You might be happy touching the drips of piss and fucking cheesy bits from his knob end that he's wiping all over the place but I'm fucked if I am." said Charlie.

Point taken, we all had a good freshen up and made sure we washed our hands before leaving and I had a little chuckle to myself as the others all made their way up the stairs without laying a finger on the handrail.

After a good breakfast in one of Grimsby's finest greasy spoons we walked back to the football ground for a look around. Being so far away from kick off time there were no police around and the exit gates at one end were wide open so we decided to have a look inside. As we wandered onto the edge of the pitch we were stopped by what I presume was the groundsman, although he looked more like something that had just crawled out of a hole in the ground. He was fat and ugly with hairs sprouting from several huge warts on his chin and saliva dribbling from the corners of his mouth. He ambled over towards us and told us we couldn't go onto the playing surface. Just as he stopped us we heard a shout from behind us and looked around to see two fellow fans who had also taken to doing away matches for the weekend. One of the lads was known as Giddy Bill, because he was giddy and his name was Bill!! The other was known as Johnny Rotten because of his remarkable ability to throw up at will. This had made him a huge hit with all the punk rockers a couple of years earlier and had got him barred from just about every pub and club back home.

Giddy Bill and Johnny joined us by the side of the pitch and Johnny took one look at the groundsman, called him an ugly bastard and spewed up onto his precious playing surface. Not wanting to hang around the pile of chopped carrots and other assorted half-digested lumps of food we made a swift exit from the ground and headed back for the main road that linked Grimsby and Cleethorpes. Giddy Bill told us how they had come down the previous night on the pay train but avoided paying by dodging in and out of toilets as the conductor did his rounds.

"Don't they check the toilets?" asked Jimmy.

"Only if you shut the door," Said Bill "if you leave it open and stand behind it the thick bastards think it's empty."

"Where did you stay last night?" Charlie asked.

"In a bed and breakfast in Cleethorpes,'" said Johnny "didn't pay for that either, they're half empty at this time of year so if you wander in about half nine and go straight to a room nobody bothers you. The locks are easy to pick and they're usually watching the telly and don't notice you come in. Then in the morning we slipped out down the fire escape while the landlady was making breakfast."

"Mind you she'll think fucking Goldilocks has been when she checks the room," said Bill "who's been spewing in my bed." he added with a laugh.

Stacey baulked at the thought and I could have sworn Charlie was looking round for somewhere to wash his hands.

Bill and Johnny decided to go down into Grimsby and we declined to join them saying we had just been, adding that we would probably see them later but hoping that we wouldn't. It was this type of moron that I was so desperate not to become and the less I associated with them the better.

Charlie told us that the sole was coming off his shoe and that he needed something to fix it so we wandered along until we found a newsagents shop and went inside to see if they had any glue.

"We've got better than glue," said the proprietor "we've got *Super glue*, It's been on the telly."

"Thora fucking Hird's been on the telly, that doesn't mean she's any fucking good." said Charlie, ever the cynic.

"I'll tell you what," said the newsagent "I'll stick your shoe for you and if it doesn't hold after two minutes you don't have to buy the glue. How's that?"

"OK." said Charlie and handed over a shoe that had been ready for the bin two years earlier but Charlie's lack of cash had enforced several botched up repairs to extend its life span.

Charlie stood with his big toe poking out of the hole in his sock and watched as the newsagent cleaned up the offending area of sole with a small piece of sandpaper and applied a couple of spots of clear glue from a tiny tube. He then pressed the shoe against the counter bringing the two separate pieces together giving a commentary as he worked.

"It's important that whatever is being glued is clean, dry and free from dust," he said sounding like someone off Blue Peter "and you must make sure you don't get any glue on your skin, It sticks like shit to a blanket and it's a hospital job to get it off." he went on, a little less Blue Peter like.

Charlie's eyes lit up and, as the newsagent handed back the shoe, Charlie had already decided he was having the glue before he had chance to test the repair.

"Pay for a tube of that fucking glue mate." he said to Stacey as if it were natural that he should pick up the bill for anything that took Charlie's fancy. To my continued amazement Stacey got out his wallet and paid what seemed an extortionate price for such a small tube of glue no matter how super it was. This sister of Charlie's must be bloody amazing I thought to myself again.

From the newsagents, and with Charlie's shoes now restored to their former glory (or should that be gory), we walked the short distance up into Cleethorpes. We had a look at the beach, a bit of sand and a lot of mud being lapped by an uninviting brown sea, and crossed it off our holiday list. The Bahamas it was not.

The pubs weren't due to open for another hour so after a bit of aimless wandering we found a few shops and had a look to see if there was anything worth buying. Charlie came across a DIY shop and Stacey provided the funds for a pack of wet and dry sandpaper and we all went outside and watched, intrigued, as Charlie proceeded to rub one side of a ten pence piece. He then led us into a sweet shop and asked the shopkeeper for ten assorted penny chews. As the shopkeeper selected and wrapped the chews in a paper bag Charlie took out his super glue and placed a drop onto the ten pence piece pressing it into the shopkeepers hand in exchange for the sweets. We all hurried out of the shop as the shopkeeper went over to the till and started shouting and swearing as he attempted to release the coin which had stuck instantaneously to the palm of his hand.

"Fucking brilliant stuff this," said Charlie holding up the glue "hours of fucking fun here."

"I think I should use some on my wallet before he bleeding empties it." said Stacey showing the first signs of dissent towards Charlie.

As opening time grew closer we went to the station by the sea front and welcomed more of our fans as their trains arrived. We then managed to work our way around most of the pubs that had decided to open and weren't manned by doormen turning visiting supporters away. Apart from the odd shouting match and a brief flurry of activity when a few Grimsby fans appeared and were quickly chased off by a few Blades we didn't run into any real trouble although we did hear of a couple of pubs being turned over nearer to the ground.

I'll give it to the Grimsby fans they always showed up when we were in town.

At a quarter to three we arrived at the ground and after some queuing found ourselves stuck in a corner of the ground designed to hold about a thousand less fans than were crammed in. Charlie made the most of the cramped conditions by gluing two men's coats together but didn't get to see the results as neither man could move far enough for anything to happen.

The match was another huge disappointment and we ended up losing four nil and what had started out a season full of promise with us widely tipped as promotion favourites ended up fizzling out into mid table mediocrity. To make matters worse Grimsby had won the title and we had to suffer their celebrations for good measure. The worst thing of all was that the Pigs had managed to sneak into a promotion place and we were never going to hear the last of it. Even so at the end of the match four thousand of our supporters refused to leave the ground until our team came back out onto the pitch. They were greeted like *they* were the champions and, getting caught up in the ludicrously misplaced triumphant atmosphere they threw their shirts into the crowd. I was quick enough to grab one from the air and improved my fiscal situation by immediately selling it to some fool beside me for £20. We had just finished a disastrous second half to our first ever season in the third division and were going off like we had won the European Cup. God knows what would happen if our lot ever actually won something.

Once out of the ground we made our way swiftly back towards Skegness. We decided not to push our luck by parking on the same caravan site again so instead we headed back to Stacey's parents caravan and from a distance checked to see if by some chance Stacey's mum and step dad had left. Our luck was out but, knowing the setup, Stacey managed to get us a key to the shower block where we all managed to get scrubbed up and changed into fresh clothes for the evening.

Charlie suggested breaking into an empty caravan, but most of the caravans were now either occupied or overlooked so we resigned ourselves to another night in the car and headed for the entertainment centre at Ingoldmels. Entertainment centre was probably pushing it a bit far as a description of the two pubs, chip shop and night club was concerned but it was close to the caravan site, so I didn't have to drive and therefore could have a skin full if I wanted. Our spirits were then lifted when we saw posters advertising a special bank holiday disco for that Saturday night.

After a good fish and chip meal we spent an unusually quiet evening, by our standards, flitting between the two pubs and I was pleasantly surprised by both the age and amount of people around the area. I had been expecting a load of grumpy old caravan club types playing dominoes and cribbage and was delighted by the sight of a couple of busloads of locals, mainly girls in their late teens and early twenties arriving for the disco. Apparently there was a bit of a Mod revival going on and Skegness was full to overflowing with spotty Parka clad youths running riot. Most pubs and clubs were either too full to get through the doors or shut up from fear of damage just before the start of the holiday season, so a lot of the locals were heading for the outskirts for the night. This left us with the dilemma of whether we should go for a bit of action with the Mods or have a crack at the other sort of action with the local talent. No contest, the Mods could wait.

Charlie had been experimenting with his super glue with mixed success. He managed to glue a glass to a table top, which caused the glass collector to upset everything else on the table as he tried to pick up the glass. This earned the pot man a bollocking from the landlord and us a round on the house as neither the landlord nor the glass collector had any idea what had been the cause of the accident. But Charlie had failed in his attempts to build a tower with four lager bottles, as he could not get the bottles dry enough for the glue to stick properly. He also managed to stick his fingers together twice and struggled to get them apart for a few minutes but the newsagent's tale of having to go to hospital for treatment seemed a bit far-fetched. A good tug separated the offending digits leaving nothing more than a bit of redness and some hard patches of skin/glue, which Charlie attempted to wash off at least five times in an hour without success.

At ten thirty we went into the night club which was an unimaginatively designed place with a central dance floor, tables and chairs around the edges and a bar at one end. The lighting was classic seventies flashing everything and the compulsory mirror covered ball dangled from the ceiling. The music was middle of the road rubbish and the volume was low enough so you could hold a conversation without having to shout. All in all it appeared to be shite. The one saving grace was that there must have been at least two girls for every bloke in the place and what blokes there were looked like they would not be much of a threat if we started getting giddy.

We sat at a table right next to the dance floor, which was a departure from our normal sit in a corner to see what was coming tactics, but we didn't feel threatened and it gave us the best view of the local talent strutting their stuff around their handbags. Out of the four of us only Jimmy had ever been one for dancing and he preferred head banging to hand jiving so we all remained seated watching the writhing bodies and bouncing bosoms in front of us. Jimmy who had been sat silently watching the dance floor for some time then pointed out that every time someone went on the dance floor and did something slightly different it took about thirty seconds for most of the others to start copying the move.

"I bet if someone got up and started squirming around like a daft twat they'd all do the same." said Jimmy.

"I can squirm around like a daft twat." said Charlie and got up onto the dance floor.

"That's because you are a daft twat." mumbled Stacey to himself.

None of us had ever seen Charlie dance before so we weren't sure how much over the top he was going, but I'd never seen anything like it. Charlie planted both feet firmly on the floor close together, bent his knees slightly and wiggled slowly from the hips and shoulders then started slowly waving his arms around his head like someone drowning in slow motion, all the time pulling a face like he had just sucked a lemon. We all pissed ourselves laughing as three or four idiots around him started to do the same. We then stopped suddenly as he was joined in his dopey dance by a gorgeous young bird with long blonde hair, long shapely legs and tits like melons, the whole package just about contained in her skin tight top and satin trousers.

It wasn't long before Charlie and the girl eased their way off the dance floor and into a quiet corner of the club where, to our amazement, they sat talking for over five minutes without the girl slapping Charlie and storming off. Stacey decided that what worked for Charlie could work for him and dashed for the dance floor and started cavorting in a fashion that made Charlie's routine look like Fred Astaire. We all pissed ourselves again when everyone within ten yards of Stacey moved off the dance floor giving him looks like he was a lump of dog shit they had just stood in. Stacey came back over to our table looking sheepish and we didn't help by pretending we didn't know him.

I noticed Charlie's bird go over to the toilets and Charlie came over and told us that he was going to take the girl outside in a few minutes and that we should not wait for him. As Charlie left us I told Jimmy that the chance of seeing Charlie in action with this girl was too good an opportunity to miss and so we decided to go outside and spy on him. This may seem a bit of a dirty trick to play on a mate but you have to understand that this is a bloke whose idea of sophisticated conversation with women normally runs to *'Nice tits love'* and *'Do you fuck?'* Which is why he usually gets far more slaps than shags and we were intrigued.

We slipped out of the club while Charlie was waiting for the girl to return from the toilet and hid behind a large van on the car park outside. After what seemed like forever, and after Jimmy pointed out that if Charlie had blown it with the girl we would all have to pay again to re-enter the club, Charlie appeared arm in arm with the girl and they headed for the road that ran along the other side of the club.

After skirting quietly around the club, peeping around the corners to make sure the coast was clear; we followed Charlie and the girl until they eventually stopped at a phone box beside a bus shelter and stood talking. The road we were on was about ten feet above the surrounding caravan site, as were most of the roads in the area, and there was a sloping grass bank from the footpath down to the site below. Stacey, Jimmy and I ran down the slope about fifty yards further up the road from Charlie and stealthily crept along the banking until we were directly behind him. We strained to hear what Charlie was saying but could not make out any words so we crawled

113

on our hands and knees to the top of the bank, struggling to stifle the giggles which would have given the game away.

Whatever inroads Charlie had been making with the girl it sounded like he had just blown it because as we got within earshot we could here Charlie saying "I've not brought you out here for fuck all, you could at least let me have hold of your tits you tight bitch."

Back to normal I thought. The girl who by now had realised that Charlie was probably not her type responded by saying "I'm sorry but I hardly know you; could you get me a taxi please I want to go home now."

I expected Charlie to tell her to get her own fucking taxi and leave her there but to my surprise he went into the phone box, picked up the handset and dialled a number. He then started speaking into the phone although there would have been no one on the other end as he had not put any money in the phone. Charlie hung up and came out of the box and said to the girl "The taxi is on its way love, are you sure I can't have a feel at you tits?"

To my astonishment the girl said, "Go on then but nothing else, I'm not that kind of a girl." As Charlie kissed the girl, who responded as though she was almost certainly that kind of a girl, and fondled her bouncing bosoms like he was kneading bread, Jimmy gestured to us to slide back down the banking. There he told me he thought it would be a laugh to get the car and make out that we were the taxi that Charlie had pretended to order, so, thinking to myself that it would never work but would surprise Charlie when a 'cab' actually turned up, I led the others quickly back to the car which was only about two hundred yards down the road.

With Stacey in the back and Jimmy in the passenger seat I drove slowly up to the bus stop and wound down the window. "Taxi." I called to Charlie expecting him to tell us to fuck off. Instead the girl opened the back door and jumped in next to Stacey with Charlie quickly following her. I expected to hear screams when the girl saw three of us in the car but she was either very drunk or very stupid because she simply tapped me on the shoulder and said "Skegness please driver." as though local taxis drove around three up all the time. Going along with the ruse I pulled out and headed for Skegness. In the rear view mirror I could see Charlie and the girl doing some serious tonsil wrestling and I could also see Stacey running his hands all over her breasts. The girl didn't seem to be objecting and I thought surely she must have known it was not Charlie's hands feeling her up. I gave Jimmy a nudge and he turned to check out what was happening in the back before motioning to me to pull over.

I spotted a narrow lane turning off the main road and drove along to the end, which turned out to be a small parking area overlooking the sea, and stopped the car. Charlie and the girl continued kissing for a few more seconds while Stacey carried on with his tit juggling, the whole affair was broken up when Jimmy reached over and tried to unzip the girl's trousers. I don't know if it was the fact that she really was a tits only girl or the realisation that even the most deformed Lincolnshire bumpkin could not have five hands but she suddenly sat bolt upright and shouted "No stop it."

"What's up?" said Stacey as though a young girl getting groped by three men in the back of a car was no cause for concern.

"I don't like this." said the girl.

"You must fucking love it. Jumping into the back of a car with four blokes you don't know, you must be gagging for it." Charlie said making a fresh grab for her breasts.

"Come on love drop your knickers you can have us all." said Stacey.

"I'm first." said Jimmy.

"I'm not following you, you've only just got rid of your last dose." said Stacey as though it was agreed that they were all entitled to a go at this girl.

"I'm only fourteen." said the girl causing everyone to freeze.

"Fourteen: you're kidding?" I said. I was not keen on this thing in the first place. I preferred relationships to be private and mutually agreeable but with a fourteen-year-old it was a definite non-starter in my book.

"I've had younger." said Stacey as though it was something to be proud of.

"Not in my car and not tonight," I said starting the engine. "Where can I drop you?" I asked the girl.

115

"By the clock tower in Skegness." she said, suddenly looking very young and vulnerable.

I drove into Skegness, no one speaking for the entire journey, and pulled up by the clock tower, getting out of the car to let the girl out of the back door. She clambered over Charlie who raised his hands like someone surrendering to the enemy as if to show the world that he wasn't touching the girl. As she got out and stood beside me I said quietly into her ear "In future stay away from night clubs and don't get into cars with strange men, they may not all be as nice as me."

As the girl ran off across the road I breathed a sigh of relief. It was bad enough driving about Skegness after six pints. That was taking a risk but risking getting banged up for gang raping a fourteen-year-old was something I wanted nothing to do with. I then drove back to the caravan park where we called it a night and did our best to get some sleep.

Sunday morning came and as usual on these trips it was the worst part. No one got much sleep in the car, which was much less comfortable than the old van, and we were all awake and wandering around by seven-o clock and the pubs didn't open while twelve. Charlie suggested that we could hunt some rabbits as there were plenty around, but with no nets, snares or dogs there wasn't much chance of catching one so we gave him the knock back on that one and continued to wander.

Normally we used up the mornings by driving to somewhere about half way home for the Sunday dinner session but because we were staying another night there was no point driving anywhere. After about an hour of wondering what to do with ourselves Jimmy suggested walking down the beach into Skegness to get some breakfast and to see if there really were as many Mods around as we had been told the previous night. No one had any better suggestions so we set off for Skegness along the path besides the beach.

We had to walk past Butlins holiday camp and as we did Charlie took a stick from a strip of chestnut fencing where some repairs were being carried out. Charlie found a few small stones and started throwing them up and hitting them with the stick so they flew into the holiday camp. After two or three near misses he managed to hit a window causing the glass to shatter and fall to the floor. The noise alerted a security guard inside who came scurrying up to the fence shouting abuse at us to which we responded with abuse of our own directed at the guard, who was a big bugger but couldn't get outside to get at us.

The guard followed us along the fence for about thirty yards until he came to a gate. We then decided to scarper as he produced a bunch of keys and began fumbling for the right one to open the gate. I don't know if it was our reluctance to get involved in a scrap with the incredible hulk at such an early hour or the prospect of us getting imprisoned inside Butlins, perish the thought, but we did a hundred yards in record time. Even Charlie whose natural lethargy normally keeps him well away from any athletic activity was only a few yards behind. The guard, thankfully, didn't fancy the sprint and having done his bit to protect his territory retreated back into the camp presumably to prevent any of the inmates escaping before morning exercise.

After a short stop to get our breath back we continued on our way towards Skegness and as we got closer we were surprised to see so many people walking on the beach in the distance. Shortly we realised who these people were, they were Mods who had been sleeping rough overnight and who, like us, were having a wander around to pass the morning. Only they were heading out of Skegness as we were heading in. After a couple of minutes the first of the Mods were only about a hundred yards away, a group of seven all dressed up in their sad looking parkas and displaying union jack patches here, there and everywhere. In the distance there were several other groups of around the same size probably about fifty Mods in total strung out along the beach and all coming our way.

Charlie, who still had his stick, raised it to his shoulder and marched towards the first group of Mods like a soldier on parade, as he got about ten yards away, still making as though the stick was a rifle, he pointed it at the Mods and started shouting "bang, bang."

The Mods must have thought he was just some local retard and took no notice as they walked past within three feet of him and his 'rifle'. Just as they drew level Charlie altered his grip on the stick and swung it around hitting the tallest of the Mods on the back of the neck and knocking him over. He then put one foot on the prone

117

Mods back and raised the stick above his head one end in each hand and with a huge cry of "Aggression!" he jumped forwards and started swinging the stick at the other Mods who had now surrounded him.

Jimmy, Stacey and I ran the few yards across the beach to join in the affray and I drop kicked the nearest Mod just as he turned to see us coming. Jimmy dived in rugby style and took two more Mods to the ground where Stacey helped out by sticking the boot in the ribs of one as he tried to get up. The other three lost their bottle and ran back down the beach chased by Charlie with his stick.

The three Mods scrapping with Stacey, Jimmy and me put up a reasonable scrap but the surprise attack had knocked two much out of them and they soon ran off the other way leaving their mate struggling to his feet wondering what had hit him.

The other groups of Mods, seeing the punch up down the beach had by now started charging towards us. Charlie, spotting the approaching hoard, did a quick U-turn and for the second time in fifteen minutes attempted to qualify for the Olympics. On seeing the larger gang of Mods chasing Charlie back towards us we all scurried up the concrete steps from the beach to the path above. As Charlie came hurtling up the steps followed closely by two of the quicker Mods, Stacey threw a litter bin that he had ripped from its moorings down the steps sending them crashing to the beach. We then jumped over a wall into a caravan site and zig zagged between caravans towards the exit and the road beyond, glancing back to see if we were still being chased, which we were.

Outside the caravan site we could just see an open backed double decker bus pulling away from the gates. With one final sprint we managed to jump aboard before it got up too much speed. Jimmy reached out to pull Charlie on board who then collapsed onto the long seat at the rear of the bus and lit up a cigarette. As the bus pulled away we looked back to see half a dozen Mods giving up the chase by the caravan site gate.

"Fucking brilliant." said Charlie between gasps.

"Nice move Charlie," said Stacey "hundreds of Mods and only four of us so you go and play baseball with ones head."

"Well I'm a fucking rocker aren't I." said Charlie who looked the part but probably wouldn't know one end of a motorbike from the other and would have claimed to be a Mod if it had been rockers out there on the beach.

When the bus dropped us on the front in Skegness we were amazed to see so many Mods wandering around. I knew from the music charts and the success of the film Quadraphenia that there was a sort of mini revival going on but this was like going back to Brighton in the sixties. There were scooters with dozens of mirrors on parked all the way along the promenade. Gangs of parka clad youths wandered around displaying embroidered patches proclaiming their origins such as 'Scunthorpe Mods', 'York Scooter Club', 'Lincoln Lamberetta Society'. There were groups from all over the east of England assembled on the Lincolnshire coast and no one was fighting. I said to Jimmy "If these were football fans there would be a riot."

"If someone turns up on a motorbike wearing leather there might be." he replied.

"We're not exactly dressed like Gerry and the fucking Pacemakers ourselves." said Charlie pointing out that our clothes didn't exactly blend in.

"I don't know," said Stacey "I think I look pretty smart myself."

He was the only one of us not wearing jeans.

"Well put a fucking parka on and fuck off with you Mod mate's then." said Charlie.

"I might just do that; at least they won't bleed me dry." Stacey said, his rebellion growing.

"O shut up fucking moaning and find us a pub." said Charlie deciding not to cut off his meal ticket just yet, although I wondered just how much longer Stacey would fall for it.

Fortunately it was almost opening time and as we got towards the far end of the promenade near the clock tower there was a great rush of bodies across the road as The Jolly Fisherman opened its doors for business. We joined the throng and scrambled over the mass of crash helmets piled high in the entrance hall and stood for at least fifteen minutes waiting to get served. The Mods were all well behaved and it seems they were more bent on music than mayhem which I was pleased about seeing as though there must have been at least two hundred of them in that one pub alone.

Charlie, resigned to the fact that he wasn't going to be scrapping with anybody this lunch time, occupied his mind by gluing as many crash helmets together as he could. I watched as he tried lifting one up and at least three others came with it. After he had glued a few helmets he started work on any other oddments he could find including a leather handbag belonging to a well-dressed young woman in her mid-twenties which he glued to a stool. I had noticed the young woman and her two friends all of whom were reasonably good looking, but appeared to be a bit too stuck up for my taste. I wondered who they might be because, like us, they were dressed differently from the majority in the pub and I wondered about three young women apparently unaccompanied in a pub at Sunday lunch time. Either lesbians or on the game I was thinking to myself as one of them got up and reached for the handbag on the stool. As she attempted to pick up the bag the weight of the attached stool dragged it from her hand and the stool toppled over spilling the contents of the bag onto the floor. Being closest I quickly got up and went over to help pick up the contents of the bag, seeing it as an opportunity to try for a pull. (Not being my type didn't stop me from giving it a go). I gathered up a lipstick tube and what looked like a small diary or address book and then, noticing a small leather wallet type of thing picked it up and glanced at what looked at first like a bus pass. As I handed it over I said loud enough for the others to hear "Here you are officer, you nearly lost your warrant card."

"I suppose you've no idea who's responsible for this little trick have you?" asked the WPC.

"What trick is that?" I asked, feigning ignorance, as Charlie slipped out of the door behind us.

"I think you know what trick, but I'll not be able to prove it will I?" She said.

"Probably not, but we could go somewhere private so you can question me darling." I replied.

"You'd like that wouldn't you?" she said, and I'm sure I saw a glint in her eye.

"Only if you were off duty and I got the chance to use the handcuffs." I said looking her straight in the eye with my best '*come to bed*' stare.

Her eyes returned the look and I was sure there was something going on inside, but before she had chance to respond a shout of "Oi! copper has your truncheon got batteries?" came from over my shoulder from some idiot Mod on a nearby table and the moment was gone. I got up to leave, deciding that I better not push my luck any further as there were forced to be more plain clothes coppers around, but as I walked away I gave her a wink which she returned with a smile before getting to grips with the task of trying to separate her handbag from the stool. I beckoned to Jimmy and Stacey to go and we left the pub before the policewoman decided that we were responsible after all.

We looked around and eventually found Charlie who was hiding behind the big wooden Jolly Fisherman sign out on the footpath.

"What were you doing trying to chat up a copper?" asked Stacey with a disgusted look on his face "I'd rather shag a scabby dog." he went on.

"She's just a woman," I said "and from what I've heard scabby dogs are about all you can pull"

"I get my share." Stacey snapped back.

I couldn't resist the opportunity to wind him up some more,

"Yeah a share's about all you get, you can't pull for yourself."

"I'll show you who can pull tonight," said Stacey "I bet I can pull a bird before you do."

"Tell you what," I said "I'll make it easy for you; we can have a goat contest so you can operate at your usual level."

"What's a fucking goat contest?" asked Charlie.

"It's where you have to go out and pull the ugliest bird you can find." explained Jimmy.

"That scrawny bastard's forced to win. I've only ever seen him with slappers." said Charlie pointing at Stacey.

"Are you saying your sisters a slapper?" asked Stacey.

"No I'm not and you better not either or I'll kick your fucking head in." replied Charlie "You've not been with my fucking sister except in your fucking dreams, she'd not go with you if you were the last bloke on earth and had a diamond studded Dick. She thinks you're a total fucking tosser. She told me she's fed up with you hanging around her and if *I* don't fucking smack you soon, she will." He went on with a passion that didn't seem natural for a brother sister relationship, at least based on my own experience, maybe it was just me who didn't get on too well with my sister.

"She never said that," said Stacey "I know she fancies me."

I know which version I believed.

Before the conversation could degenerate any further our attention was grabbed by the sound of shouting voices coming from inside the pub. It seemed that someone had discovered the heap of glued helmets and it was all about to kick off. We walked quickly along the front and the nipped down into a park which led firstly to blocks of guest houses and then to the main road up the coast. We caught a bus back to the caravan site and arrived just in time to spot Stacey's mum and step dad loading their luggage into their car and heading for home. We watched as the car drove off and when they were safely out of view Stacey collected the caravan key from the site office and we finally got into our planned accommodation.

Stacey's caravan soon started looking like a pig sty. We cooked a meal between us and I knew no one was going to offer to clean the pots and pans or clear out the food wrappers and other bits of litter that seemed to appear from nowhere. Stacey would probably get another kicking when his step father found out, but by now I was getting fed up of him and I didn't care one way or another.

After another shower and change of clothes we headed back into Skegness for the evening and set out the rules for the goat contest. The rules were simple, we would split into pairs and at nine o clock we had to meet up in the Sun Castle pub on the sea front with the ropiest old dogs we could pull. The winner would get his drinks bought by the others for the rest of the evening. Charlie said he liked the idea of being the winner.

"If there are free fucking drinks involved I'll kidnap some old crow if I have to." he said.

"They've got to be both consenting and conscious to count." said Jimmy

"Fucking spoil sport." replied Charlie.

"And no school children please." I said looking at Charlie

"What about Stacey's mother, She's an ugly bastard and she's no fucking schoolgirl." he replied.

"Fuck off." said Stacey as we all rolled about laughing, Charlie had got a point.

We split into two pairs, Stacey and Charlie heading off one way and Jimmy and me going the other. While Stacey and Charlie went off in search of ugly birds Jimmy and me went round to the Jolly Fisherman as we had previously arranged and laughed at the thought of the other two spending their evening chatting up dogs. We stayed in the pub while about half eight talking about previous experiences and making plans for the next season's campaign and then made our way to the Sun Castle ready to meet the other two.

Just before nine the door opened and Charlie came in dragging a scruffy looking girl behind him. She wasn't the best looking girl in the world but I'd seen worse. Having said that Charlie was welcome to her, I wouldn't have touched her with a barge pole.

"Two fucking halves love." he barked at the barmaid from half way across the room. The barmaid served him without a flinch and he came over and sat beside us looking puzzled to find us on our own.

"Fuck me." he said realising he had been stitched up and then stopped before he gave the game away completely. The scruffy girl looked at us and there was a sort of slow realisation that there was something not quite right going on but she hadn't quite sussed it yet. Before she had chance to ask what was going on Stacey came in with the creature from the swamp. I don't know where he had found her but if the contest was for real he had won hands down. She had the lot; she was fat, ugly, badly dressed and had make up so thick it would probably need a sandblaster to get it all off. I got up and offered her my seat, carefully positioning myself near the door ready for a quick getaway. The girl with Charlie looked at the dog that Stacey had brought in and the penny dropped.

"What's bleeding going on here?" bellowed Charlie's bird to the new arrival.

"Search me fart face," replied Stacey's wench "this lanky twat gave me a fiver to come in here with him so here I am."

123

"Well," she roared looking at Charlie "what's bleeding happening?"

"It's her." he said pointing to Stacey's partner.

"What's me?" asked the swamp thing.

"You're the ugliest old fucking goat in Skegness and she isn't far behind." he replied.

"I know," swamp thing shouted after us as we made a swift exit "but I'm a fiver better off for it."

As we ran down the steps back onto the street we could hear the shouting and cursing coming from inside and I thought it was a good job they were too fat to run after us because if they caught us we were dead meat. Stacey tried to claim his prize but we told him where to get off, apart from the fact that we had been playing a prank on him, paying for it was never part of the deal.

"But I'm down to my last few quid now and there's hours to go yet." he moaned.

"You should have fucking thought of that when you paid that dog." said Charlie.

"Don't you get so smart," said Stacey "you're going to have to buy your own now."

"Bollocks," said Charlie "I've only got two quid to last me a fucking week."

So at a quarter past nine on a Sunday night we were in the middle of Skegness with Stacey and Charlie almost skint and I hadn't been paid for the petrol yet.

Jimmy decided that he was not going to buy everybody drinks all night and I certainly wasn't so it was every man for himself which meant Stacey and Charlie would have to severely pace themselves.

Feeling a bit down we headed for another pub and found ourselves at The Ship on the corner of the main coast road. Having got myself a drink I decided to bring up the subject of petrol money. Jimmy was good as gold and paid his share without question Charlie just looked at Stacey who in turn said he hadn't enough left to cover it and asked if he could pay his share when we got back. Against my better judgement I said he could but I wanted paying within a week and I wanted the money for both Stacey and Charlie. If they had a disagreement it was between the two of them and I had brought them on the understanding that Stacey was paying for two. Reluctantly Stacey agreed and I wondered to myself how long it would take to get my money and how much longer Charlie would be sponging off Stacey.

I downed my pint and went back to the bar for a refill, as we were now all buying our own. I was joined at the bar by Charlie who produced a pound and informed me that that was the last of his money before ordering a half of bitter from the barmaid. As I turned away from the bar all hell let loose. The barmaid had only given Charlie change from fifty pence and not the pound he had given her and she was swearing that she had only been given fifty pence. Charlie was just swearing. He then grabbed the barmaid by the front of her blouse and was trying to drag her over the bar. Two locals grabbed Charlie and were trying to drag him off the barmaid and Jimmy grabbed the two locals by the hair and was trying to drag them off Charlie. Stacey was preventing any one else getting near the scene by waving a pool cue at those who came within reach. I was stood looking at the whole surreal affair laughing and thinking it reminded me of the children's story about the giant turnip, then the whole bunch of them suddenly gave way and they all ended up in a heap on the floor. The barmaid remained on the other side of the bar with her blouse ripped open and her bra on show to the whole pub, most of who were shouting for more.

The landlord of the pub had by now appeared from wherever he kept himself and was enquiring as to what was going on. Charlie continued growling and swearing and I intervened and explained that the barmaid had short changed Charlie by fifty pence. I thought it sounded ridiculous now when looking at the scene, but I suppose when fifty pence is the sum of your wealth, as was the case with Charlie, then it was something to fight over. The landlord didn't agree and said that if Charlie had been short changed it would show up on the till and he would have to come back the following morning to find out. For good measure he told us that if we didn't leave the pub in two minutes he would phone the police and report Charlie's attack on his staff. Much to Charlie's annoyance we left.

We were by this time all short of cash and getting fed up. This was the longest time we had spent as a group on one of our away trips and we were starting to get a bit ratty with each other. We decided that we would find one more pub to see out the rest of the evening and then we would get some sleep before heading for home in the morning. No night clubs, no hassle, just get through the next hour or so. It was a good enough idea but circumstances always seem to get in the way of good ideas and that night was no different.

We came across a pub just off the main road out of Skegness and wandered in not expecting to find anything out of the ordinary and at first we weren't disappointed. While Jimmy and I got the drinks in (one round only we said) Stacey and Charlie went exploring. The pub was quite large from the outside but inside it was a series of small rooms rather than one or two bigger ones which would have been more expected. By the time the drinks were sorted Charlie had come back with the news that there was a room at the rear with a pool table, so we all headed off for a game. When we entered the room we could see why Charlie had been so keen to play pool. The room had no bar, one entrance/exit and could not be properly seen from anywhere else in the pub, the only way to see what was going on was to actually go into the room. What made the room so appealing to Charlie was that it was sited bang next to the door to the cellar. By the time we had set up the pool balls and packed the pockets with empty crisp packets Charlie had 'accidentally' found his way into the cellar.

Within two minutes he wandered out with a crate of Guinness which was promptly lodged under the pool table. It looked as though our lack of cash was not going to be as big an obstacle to having a good night as we had thought. We had enough drink to last the night and with the pockets bunged up we could carry on playing pool until the pub closed without paying another penny. The biggest problem now seemed to be that closing time was approaching faster than we wanted but this problem solved itself when the barman popped his head around the door and asked Jimmy if we were OK for a shut in. We couldn't believe our luck and Jimmy showed willing by ordering another round just so the bar staff didn't start to twig on to the cellar scam. Just to rub it in Charlie said he was going to the toilet and appeared two minutes later with a bottle of Southern Comfort from the cellar. Charlie said he just had a poor sense of direction and it seemed a waste to come back up all those stairs empty handed.

After god knows how many free games of pool and a right skin full of free booze and just when we thought it was going to be the perfect end to our weekend it all went shit shaped again. Two of the locals from one of the other rooms decided that they wanted to play pool. Half past one in the morning and all of a sudden they want to play pool! Jimmy and I had just about had enough of bloody pool anyway and would probably have given up the table but instead of just asking, these loud-mouthed Lincolnshire tossers decided they were going to try and make us move.

Stacey was the first to react for once and before the locals had finished telling us to fuck off out of their pub he had smashed the cue ball into the forehead of the nearest one sending him staggering back through the doorway into the passage. Charlie then transformed into Fatima fucking Whitbread and launched a cue 'javelin' style at the other one sending him running for cover.

This did two things, on the plus side it bought us a few seconds time to get sorted. On the minus side it caused such a commotion that it alerted everyone in the pub to the fact that there were four outsiders causing a fuss trapped in a small room with nowhere to go, which was not good news.

Jimmy realised our predicament and quickly slammed the door shut before any of the locals could get in, and between us we managed to drag the pool table across and barricade the door. We looked around and the only way out appeared to be through a small opening casement in the window that was barely big enough to get a head through never mind the rest of our bodies. Not good.

While we listened to the banging at the door and pondered on how we might get out in one piece Charlie solved our problem. There was a curtain hanging the full height of the room in one corner to the side of the window and when Charlie looked behind it he found a fire exit door so we all dashed out of the fire exit and scurried off into the darkness. When we were suitably clear of the pub we stopped to consider our next move.

"The fucking cops will be all over here in five minutes." said Charlie.

"Don't talk daft," said Jimmy "they're not likely to phone the coppers and say they've had a bit of trouble during an after bird session are they?"

"You're right," I said "but we don't want that crowd of pissed up carrot crunchers on our backs though do we?"

"No, I've had enough of this place for a while I reckon we should set off for home now instead of the morning." said Stacey.

No one argued so we all headed back for the car and although I was well over the limit for driving, the events of the evening had left me felling sober as a judge so I started up the car and set off for home with a feeling of relief.

We headed back towards Skegness and as I was about to take a right turn and head for home Charlie suddenly started going mental in the back, Shouting and screaming for me to stop. I thought he must have got his leg out of the door dragging down the road or something from the fuss he was making so I pulled up and asked him what was wrong.

"I've not got my fucking change from that bastard landlord have I?" he said.

"For fucks sake Charlie I thought it was something serious." I replied.

"It is fucking serious" he said, "That's all I've got for the rest of the fucking week"

"Go on, let's go back for it," said Jimmy "I want to see that bastards face when we knock him up for fifty pence."

So we went back to the pub and knocked and banged until the landlord came to the door and it was well worth the delay to see the look of disbelief on his face when Charlie demanded fifty pence at two forty five in the morning. The landlord was so stunned he went inside and came back with a coin and handed it over without saying a single word. Charlie took the coin kissed it and said "Thank you and good fucking night." to the landlord and walked off whistling '*I'm in the money*' as loud as he could.

We arrived back home at five o clock in the morning and I felt like we'd been gone a month. These trips were all right but they started to take their toll after a while. I for one was glad the football season was over and I could have a break to recharge the batteries. I dropped Stacey off last and as he got out I said "Petrol money; one week." with enough of a hinted threat to get the message over. I then went home to bed and slept all day.

Chapter 11

CLOSED SEASON

No Games

The following weekend I met up with Jimmy and Charlie and we watched the F.A. Cup final in our local pub but at that time I found it hard to get too involved in a match as a neutral and we ended up coming out before the end.

Stacey still hadn't paid me for the petrol and so we decided to give him a call. Stacey's step dad answered the door and when we asked for Stacey he said,

"The little runt told me to tell you he was working but he's not really, he's down the bookies."

What a bastard, I thought. I wasn't happy that Stacey was avoiding having to pay what he owed but grassing him up was still a shit trick. Nevertheless we all headed for the bookmakers and inside there was Stacey sat in the corner studying form. He looked a bit surprised to see us but soon recovered and gave us all the usual bullshit about how he'd tried to ring but couldn't get through etc. etc.

"Fuck that," I said, "where's my ten quid?"

"I wanted to see you about that," he said "I'm a bit short at the moment and I wondered if I could have another week."

"A bit fucking short," I said ripping the newly written betting slip from his hand "a bit short and you're writing out bets for twenty quid on a fucking dog race, you're taking the piss."

"That bets not for me it's for someone else." whimpered Stacey.

"Well you can owe the money to someone fucking else then." I said and grabbed the twenty pound note out of Stacey's other hand.

"Give it back you bastard." said Stacey.

"I'll show you what a bastard is." I said and grabbed Stacey by the collar and pushed him through the door to the gents.

Once inside I gave him one with the head right on the bridge of his nose causing an immediate nose bleed and pushed him roughly into a toilet cubicle where he stumbled and fell, ending up wedged between the toilet pan and the cubicle wall. Before he could get up I stamped my foot into his face stunning him and then I ripped the toilet seat off the pan and threw it hoop-la style over his head. I walked out of the toilet rubbing my hands and shouted over my shoulder as I left "Now that's a bastard for you."

"What have you done to him?" Asked Jimmy who had stayed outside the toilet keeping prying eyes away while I sorted Stacey.

"I've just showed him the importance of paying his debts on time." I said with a smile.

"I don't think we'll be seeing much of him from now on," I added "come on I'll treat you to a couple of drinks seeing as though I'm a tenner up on the deal."

So off we went to the nearest pub and that was the last we saw of Stacey.

We continued meeting up at weekends and passing the time with several daft tricks and hare-brained schemes like scrounging scrap from the local tip (Charlie's idea) or the night we went poaching trout from a breeding pool and ended up getting shot at by the water bailiff, but it wasn't the same as the football matches. It's funny but when I was on the trips I was usually glad to get back but once they stopped I missed them and couldn't wait for them to start again. I suppose I knew that there must be more to life than the football. I just hadn't found out what yet. What I did know was that closed season was boring.

I spent more time with my girlfriend and I began to feel trapped and confused. I had always had plans to settle down but it appeared to be coming too quickly and I wasn't sure I was ready for it yet. Somewhere inside I started to wonder whether I was missing out on something and I began to look around for what that was.

I had a brief fling with a woman I had met while working at her house and during the time I was with her managed to break my hand punching a bouncer who had offended her. This led to me being off work and while I was off I went to see Charlie's latest appearance in the Crown Court where he got 150 hours community service for assault causing actual bodily harm. It was during this court case that I met Charlie's sister for the first time. Wow!!! I instantly understood why Stacey had been so keen. I was sat with Jimmy in the public gallery at the back of the court when this amazing looking bird came in and sat on the row behind us. From what I saw in that first brief glance I knew she ticked all the right boxes in my book. To make things even better she convinced me she was no snob (remember my indifference to posh birds) when she leaned over and whispered into my ear.

"If they send him down I reckon we jump the barrier and have the judge."

I remember agreeing and at the same time praying that Charlie did not get sent down. There was no way I was having a go at a judge.

During the interval for lunch Jimmy, Charlie's sister and I went to a nearby pub for a drink. I had gathered from Stacey's actions around Charlie that his sister must have been a bit special. I'd also had prior warning that she did not like being chased so, feigning indifference, I chatted to her about Charlie and tried to appear to not be amazingly attracted to her and the result was that she started chasing me. I was flattered and frankly amazed and for a couple of weeks I juggled Charlie's sister, my long term girlfriend and the woman from work. It was a mad time and cumulated in my girlfriend finding out I had spent the night of my twentieth birthday in bed with Charlie's sister and blowing me out. While it had been lots of fun it was all a bit frantic and had cost me a fortune and I was now regretting it all (except for the birthday romp with Charlie's sister, Fucking Hell!!!!) and realising that I may have blown the plans I had for a settled life.

Anyway I did a lot of creeping and apologising and eventually my girlfriend agreed to give me another chance and I don't know how it happened but somewhere along the line that summer I managed to agree to marry my girlfriend and all of a sudden I was talking about weddings and mortgages. My plans now seemed to involve curtains and three piece suites rather than punch ups and directions to Port Vale or wherever. I suppose I was suddenly growing up. So the rest of the closed season was spent making plans for where and when the big day would happen and I actually started house hunting. This was scary, I was moving from happy go lucky, fifteen pounds a week board and lodgings, loads to spend and no responsibilities, to mortgage and bills, house and garden, pipe and fucking slippers even, and I suppose I was even looking forward to it, who would have thought it!

The big downside to this was that I had agreed to no more weekends away. My girlfriend or fiancée as I suppose she now was had this understandable thing about me being away overnight so I had reluctantly agreed to stop the weekenders. I was saving like mad

134

for a deposit on a house and couldn't really afford the away games anyhow so it wasn't really a big issue. I had got a season ticket for the home games before this all blew up so they were sorted and to be honest the weekends were so fucking tiring I was ready for a break anyway.

So the next season was to be home games and the odd day trip away but no big weekends, I could live with that. We were still in the third division and the things going on at boardroom level didn't suggest an immediate end to that situation and general interest was waning. On the good news front we did have a pre-season game against Leeds at home and that was something I wasn't going to miss under any circumstance.

Chapter 12

WE HATE LEEDS

Pre season 1980/81

Blades 0 – 1 Walsall
2nd May 1981

We all fucking hate Leeds. That's how the song goes and it didn't come about without good reason. Everyone hated Leeds mostly due to Don Revie and his bunch of prima donnas, who were good, fair enough, but they were a set of dirty bastards and they used to enjoy rubbing it in. Beating teams because you're better is one thing but taking the piss is another. For every fan that Revie's team made there were a thousand lost. Too right we all fucking hate Leeds.

Actually we hated Leeds before Revie and we'll hate Leeds after Revie is just a name in history. When there are no fans left who ever actually saw a Revie side we'll still hate Leeds. It was always Leeds who got the headlines. It was always Leeds who poached our best players. It was always Leeds, Leeds, Leeds. Well now Leeds were coming to town and we could show them how we hated them.

We hadn't played them for a few years mainly because for some unfathomable reason we had found ourselves in a lower division. Many theories existed to try and explain the situation; twists of fate, biorhythmic influences, conspiracy theories all had their arguments for and against but at the end of the day it all boiled down to the fact that we were crap and had been for years.

The first time I had come across Leeds I was just entering my teens and the lasting memory of that game was three big Leeds fans cornering me and pinching my scarf. Well how fucking hard they were; not. As well as my scarf they also took our kop which at that time was an annual event for anyone with the inclination, but now times had changed and if Leeds came onto our kop this time they would get a surprise or two. Those young lads they had chased off with ease had all grown up a bit and now no one took our kop. We had seen Leeds off our kop a few years earlier and now we were after seeing them out of our city altogether. To say we were looking forward to it was an understatement.

We knew how they operated, we knew they would come early with raiding parties going for the pubs around the station and establishing a base to build up a large crew who would rampage through the town centre as kick off time grew closer. They had done it before and there was no reason to expect this time they would do anything different. Well this time they could fuck off.

The pubs opened at 11am and we knew they wouldn't start arriving much before then because if they were hanging around the streets the police would round them up and stick them on the away end of the ground straight away. We also knew which pubs they would go for because they had tended to stick to the ones that they knew from previous years where they knew the layout. So the first target was to get their favourite pubs closed.

There were two pubs close to the station that they had used before. Both older designs, small rooms, narrow corridors multiple entrances and exits. Hard to spot an enemy build up if they did it right and nearly impossible to shift them once they got in. Too many little nooks and crannies to get trapped in if it all went shit side up. Both pubs had seen trouble before, both had new landlords and both had high insurance premiums so when someone telephoned the landlords at 10.15 on Saturday morning and told them there were plans to wreck their pubs if they let Leeds fans in, it was no surprise that come 11am the doors stayed firmly shut.

With the two pubs nearest the station out of the equation it was now a case of trying to predict where they would go instead. The two pubs we had bluffed into closing were on a hill opposite the station. The second pub was almost at the top of the hill, and it was very unlikely that they would go back towards the station where they would have just had to shake off the police to get this far. When I say shake off I might be over doing it, police methods at that time were a little less advanced than nowadays. If you didn't rampage about in a mob at least thirty strong with your teams colours dangling from every limb singing 'You're going to get you fucking head kicked in' you wouldn't be recognised as a hooligan. On the other hand, thirty youths wandering up and down a hill looking lost might just get you noticed by one of the sharper coppers, even if it was just so he could show off his knowledge of the local A to Z and direct you to the nearest punch up.

So uphill they would go. From there it was left towards the football ground or right to the city centre. No contest, there was no way they would go near the ground at that time in the morning. There they would risk getting rounded up and put inside the stadium for a four hour alcohol free wait. So we set up camp in the Claymore, the first pub on the road towards the city centre and the perfect place for an ambush.

The Claymore was built in the late sixties when architects designed weird and wonderful futuristic buildings when they were high on acid and concrete boxes when they were not. The architect of the Claymore could never have heard of acid. The pub was part of a concrete block containing shops, restaurants and bars at the lower levels with offices above. Block is the perfect description, the design owing more to Lego than Leonardo.

The pub itself was rectangular shaped with a door onto the street at each end of the front wall with seating under the windows which ran the length of the wall between the doors. The fixed seating was arranged to form semi-circular booths each of which had a table in the middle and two or three loose chairs around the open side completing the circle. In the middle of the opposite wall was the bar which projected into the room in a sort of 'U' shape giving a large serving area without taking up too much of the room. At each end of the room, opposite the doors, was a staircase that led down to the toilets, Ladies one side Gents the other. Other than the seating under the windows and a few tall stools at the bar it was just one large open area of standing room only. While uninspired, this was fine for the purpose for which this pub was mainly used, which was as a meeting point for the start and finish of pub-crawls around the town. There can't have been many people in town who hadn't arranged to meet at the Claymore at some time, what it lacked in ambience it made up for in convenience. It was central for all the transport links into town. Bus, rail and taxi ranks were all within a few minutes' walk. The pubs and clubs of the town centre surrounded the place and because of its simple design it was almost impossible for anyone to enter the place without been seen by anyone inside. This also made it ideal for our purpose.

We arrived at the pub just as the landlord was opening. There was Jimmy, Malcolm and myself and we were soon joined by two of our fellow supporters who we knew from match days and could be relied on. There was a network of small groups like ours that made up the fighting force of the football club. No gang knew too much about any of the other gangs away from football but on the day of the match they would all come together to form one large army of fighting fit young men on the lookout for action.

A grapevine existed around the pubs and clubs and I was constantly amazed how a whisper here and a nod and a wink there during the week could summon a troop of warriors ready for battle on a Saturday as though everything had been planned to the last detail. I think one of the reasons the police struggled to cope in the early days is that they were looking for some Mr Big who ran the whole show. When in fact most of the biggest scraps and raids were set up on someone's whim and just escalated on the day.

Anyway the word in the week was that gangs were going to cover as many pubs as they could in small numbers from the moment they opened and as soon as anyone showed up from Leeds, runners could be sent out to summon up as many reinforcements as necessary and that's all there was to it.

We were joined after about ten minutes by Charlie who sat on the floor besides us despite there being chairs available. Charlie had not taken my liaison with his sister very well and I had only seen him a couple of times since when the only thing I could get out of him was 'You shagged my sister' over and over. It looked like I was going to get more of the same when I noticed some unfamiliar faces joining the party.

I motioned with my eyes towards the door at the top end of the room. There three youths of around seventeen years old had just walked in, the stiffness of their bodies and nervous glances around the room giving away the fact that they were strangers to town.

"We are Leeds, We are Leeds, We are Leeds." sang one of them out of nowhere pausing after the one line waiting for a reaction.

No one moved. We'd all seen this one before.

"Set up." I whispered to Jimmy while looking at Charlie from the corner of my eye. Charlie's mind seemed to have got stuck on the fact that one of his mates had had it off with his sister and he couldn't seem to see beyond that. The last thing I wanted was someone I was unsure of leading us into one of the oldest traps in the book. Charlie never moved, either he knew what the score was or he was so obsessed with the other stuff he had not even noticed. While I was trying to decide which it was, two of the Leeds fans went to the

141

bar while the other one went back outside. A few seconds later he returned accompanied by around twenty five of his bigger and older mates who had been waiting just around the corner ready to pounce on anyone foolish enough to chase the three decoys out onto the street.

As the Leeds fans streamed into the bar I noticed the odd one or two more experienced battlers glancing round the room taking in what threat there might be. What they would have seen was three lads sat by the window (us), their mate sat on the floor (Charlie) and two pairs of lads sat separately at the far end of the room, no danger apparently!

I gave a wink to a skinny lad stood alone at the opposite end of the bar from the crowd of Leeds fans. Immediately, sensing my meaning he downed the rest of his pint and walked steadily out on to the street. No one among the Leeds fans took notice of his leaving but, as they drank and the volume of their banter grew louder, the call for reinforcements was already on its way.

Moments after the skinny lad left an elderly couple entered the pub and made their way to the bar. This was not good. I figured there was about two minutes before all hell let loose in there and while I liked the idea of a good punch up, and accepted that there would be some damage caused to property, (insurance would cover the damage) I did not like the idea of this pair of innocent old dears getting caught up in something that was nothing to do with them. Besides the coppers would change tact from rounding up and moving on, to wholesale arrests and retribution if the general public got tangled up in our battle. I decided I had to act quickly so as they got to the bar I got up, went over to the couple and rounded them up swiftly whisking them back to the door and out onto the street. As I left them on the pavement I said to the bloke "Sorry we're closed."

God knows what he thought but he looked at me, looked at his wife and tottered off down the street good as gold.

As I re-entered the Claymore all eyes were on me. The Leeds fans previously oblivious to the threat and growing in confidence had sussed us out. They had about a minute left before reinforcements arrived and if they had waded straight in they could have had us and been away, but they were a bunch of tossers. Instead of laying in and giving us a good pasting they started singing "We are Leeds, we are Leeds, we are Leeds." and motioning to us with their hands to come and have a go. Stupid twats, we *were* going to have a go that's why we were there. Charlie, who was by now on his feet, decided he had heard enough and picked up an ashtray from the table throwing it hard at the group from Leeds who ducked as one and the ashtray crashed against the wall. If the Leeds fans had been unsure of our intentions before, they had just been given a bit of a clue and responded by charging towards us to be met by kicks punches and the odd table and chair swung at various parts of their anatomy. I don't know why but in situations like this, that usually last for a matter of seconds, everything seems to go so slowly and the brain seems to take in every detail of what is going on all around. I can clearly remember noticing, in the midst of the mayhem that was going on, a few of the less enthusiastic Leeds fans making a bolt for the door to be greeted by the first of the reinforcements as dozens of our lads from the pub across the road just waded in.

As the furore continued there came a point where the rest of the Leeds fans must have decided they were onto a loser and they made a bolt for it, most of them making it through the doors but receiving a good kicking from our lot on the way. The last three seeing the ranks of opposition closing across the door in front of them turned and made a dash for the stairs behind them, presumably expecting a rear exit but only finding the gents toilet at the bottom of the stairs.

The whole place suddenly went quiet, the silence only broken by the booming voice of a giant, known to all as Garth, who was thankfully on our side.

"Those three are mine." he said and strolled down the stairs towards the toilet. The rest of the crowd remained at the top of the stairs listening to the bang, bang, bang as Garth gave the three Leeds fans his own particular welcome to town. Seconds later Garth reappeared with a smile on his face and someone shouted out

"What happened?"

"Fucking shit themselves." said Garth

"Well they're in the right place." said a voice from the mob which was greeted with a cheer from the laughing crowd.

With the business now over I turned to survey the scene inside the Claymore and could not believe my eyes. As I looked around I saw in the middle of the mess that was left, where every table, chair, stool, glass, ashtray and any other loose object had been thrown, swung, kicked over or otherwise destroyed, there in the middle of all that carnage stood Charlie holding a full pint of beer with not a drop spilled.

"How did you manage that?" I asked, amazed.

"Got to be fucking careful with your beer haven't you," said Charlie "you don't know where the fucking next one's coming from."

Before I had chance to think of a reply to that our party was broken up by the sound of police sirens approaching (why do they do that). This was our signal to split up and merge in with the crowd of Saturday shoppers outside before moving on to our next port of call. As we went around the town centre we heard several stories similar to our own where the Leeds fans had been kicked out of the pubs before they had chance to establish a foothold. By half past two most had given up trying to take our pubs and headed to the ground where they had been shepherded onto the end of the ground allocated to away supporters. This meant that our kop was under no threat of being taken but also meant that we would not get the pleasure of kicking off any invaders and enhancing our reputation among the hooligan classes.

With the adrenaline still flowing and our confidence high after our successes we somehow managed to come up with the stupid idea of taking the battle to Leeds by going on the away end ourselves. This was not a normal tactic against the likes of Leeds. Although we hated them we had to admit to having a certain amount of respect for their reputation and while we would battle to hold our own territory against invasion we would normally draw the line at going for a full strength away crew of the size Leeds could usually muster. This day bolstered by a combination of a feeling of invincibility gained from our earlier adventures and a belief in some half drunken reasoning that, as this was only a pre-season game, Leeds would not be at full strength we decided that they were there for the taking.

We had been on the away end often enough in the past and the plan was simple and well tried. We would enter the ground in ones and twos usually tagged onto the end of a bunch of away fans that would be quickly ushered through the turnstiles by the police who were more concerned about getting visitors off the street than trying to spot any infiltration. Once inside we would form into small groups and gather in various spots around the edge of the main group of away fans and see how the land lay before making a move. If the away fans were poorly represented a quick verse of one of our team's songs would alert them to our presence and more often than not send them scurrying off into a corner to watch the match in shame, (the area directly behind the goal being the prize position). Occasionally there would be some resistance and the odd minor scuffle would ensue before either one side would yield or the police would separate the two sides and if the home supporters' presence was only small in numbers they would be transferred to their own end. Either way there was not usually any great risk attached to going on the away end. You either got to chase off a bunch of wimps or had a quick scuffle and were taken around the edge of the pitch to your mates and gained a few seconds of glory as you were cheered home.

This day we realised that we had misjudged the situation. As soon as we got through the turnstiles we found the end to be packed to overflowing with thousands of Leeds fans many of whom had been given a good beating in town and were not in the best of moods. Jimmy and I had gone in together with a bunch of young, noisy but otherwise harmless Leeds fans and, surprised by the size of the crowd, had headed at once for the pie stall. This was a usual meeting place as anyone hanging around would look as though they were waiting for refreshments rather than trouble.

Charlie and Malcolm were already there and I noticed three more of our lot about ten yards away looking rather nervous. I flicked them a glance and indicated to them to head for the front of the terracing and said to Jimmy as we attempted to push our way carefully through the crowd.

"I reckon we give it a quick rush at a few at the front to let them know we're here and then let the plod take us round the other end, what do you think?"

"I'll go for that." said Jimmy who was handy enough in a scrap but sensible enough to avoid suicide missions.

"I say we have the fucking lot of 'em." growled Charlie.

"You fucking have them then." said Malcolm to Charlie who immediately had second thoughts and slithered to the front of the group of us trying to make our way to the relative safety of the front rows. About half way down we hit a snag, Charlie who was now leading us down tapped a youth on the shoulder and said "Mind your fucking backs."

I suppose it was the '*fucking*' bit that did it but instead of just moving aside to let us squeeze through, the youth turned to see who was giving it some lip. I don't know who was the most surprised, him or us, but as they faced up I recognised him as one of the youths from the Claymore and more importantly he recognised us. It was another one of those moments when time stands still for a second or so, then as the Leeds fan was wondering what to do Charlie butted him in the face sending him into reeling backwards into the crowd.

Fortunately we were still a fair bit to the side of the main Leeds mob and a lot of the Leeds fans around us were not of the fighting variety. These ordinary fans, sensing trouble, moved quickly aside leaving us stood in a gap of about five yards across with a scattering of Leeds fans squaring up around the edge ready to have us. There were about ten more steps down to the bottom of the terrace but this was now filled with Leeds fans looking up at us and braced ready for an attack. We had about five seconds before the whole lot of them realised what was going on and turned on us.

"Get 'em." I shouted to Jimmy and the rest and waded into the crowd arms and legs flailing mainly brushing against people but with the odd shot landing firmly stunning the recipient briefly. As we waded in we took a few shots but again these were mostly glancing blows and, as was usually the case, the brawl looked spectacular but no real injuries were sustained. As we fought our momentum and the weight of the now onrushing Leeds mob forced us down to the bottom of the terrace, which was where we were trying to get anyway. Once there the police jumped in and dragged us onto the track that runs around the perimeter of the pitch, giving us the odd kick or punch in the kidneys for luck. They may not admit it but I'm sure most of the police at the grounds enjoyed a good scuffle as much as the fans. We were then escorted around the pitch towards our end where we received the cheers of our supporters who from the distance had not realised that we were simply trying to escape from a badly planned and botched manoeuvre, but had seen what appeared to be a small group of their lads spectacularly and daringly attack the fully assembled forces of the mighty Leeds and we were hardly going to tell them any different were we. The downer came when instead of releasing us onto our own end the police continued to march us round the pitch and deposited us out on the street slamming the gate shut behind us and telling us not to bother coming back in or we would be arrested.

We were now outside the ground, minutes from kick off and with enough money to pay to get back in the ground or to have a drink after the match but not both. Charlie who it turns out hadn't enough money for either option then did the first useful thing he'd done all day.

"I know how we can get back in for free." he said.

"How?" we replied in unison.

"Get me a bit of fucking wood about this long." he said holding his hands about two feet apart. Curious we searched around and after a couple of minutes Malcolm came up with a piece of the same sort of fencing Charlie had used to attack the mods at Skegness.

"Fucking brilliant," said Charlie 'now follow me and when I go in you follow fucking quickly and keep on running."

We followed and watched as Charlie approached the last turnstile in a run of four, glanced inside and then ran and vaulted over the revolving barrier. The rest of us followed and as we emerged from the turnstile we saw what the wood was for. Charlie had gone in and before the turnstile attendant had realised what was happening had jammed the stick through the handles of two outwardly opening turnstile doors. This prevented either door from opening and allowed the rest of us to leap through and run into the crowd before the alarm could be raised. Once inside the ground we took up our normal positions and took the plaudits of our fellow hooligans.

Jimmy started to tell the story of how we had meticulously planned the daring raid and how he personally had took on the whole Leeds mob. I wondered how long it would be before Jimmy, Malcolm and Charlie had told the tale of how they took on all those Leeds fans so often that they started to believe their own distorted version of events. Personally I could have done without all the attention I much preferred the anonymous approach. Once you had a little notoriety it wasn't long before you had gangs of idiots wanting to be associated with you and drawing the attention of the authorities to your escapades. It would also not be long before others would try to make a challenge for what they perceived as top spot and soon we wouldn't be able to go out for a drink without some spotty sixteen year old with more bravado than brain trying to stick a glass in our faces.

This game turned out to be a template for the season with the away games being replaced by forays onto the away end of our own ground to get a bit of action and being the third division it was only a bit of action but it served a purpose.

The season turned out to be a disaster and at the final game at home to Walsall we were relegated to the fourth division when we missed a penalty in the last minute that would have saved us. We had been on the away end before the game and that manoeuvre had resulted in a good punch up in which Jimmy had received a dart in his shoulder which had been thrown by a Walsall fan. Jimmy, being Jimmy, had simply pulled the dart out and thrown it back at them but I saw it as a sign that things were changing for the worse. There was also a pitch invasion at the end where the Walsall players as well as fans got a bit of a kicking. The riot was made worse when the stadium announcer came on the tannoy to announce that other results had gone our way and we were saved from relegation. This was a total lie and within minute's fans with radios were relaying the truth and the mob turned its attention to finding the announcer, the manager, the chairman etc. and damaging much of the ground in the process. When it eventually settled down we all made our way home to contemplate the disastrous prospect of life in the fourth division.

Chapter 13

CHANGING LANES

York City 2 – 3 Blades
3rd October 1981

Port Vale 0 – 2 Blades
1oth October 1981

Northampton 1 – 2 Blades
3rd November 1981

Blades 1 – 0 Arsenal
Arsenal 2 – 0 Blades
League Cup Round One
1981-82

I had survived Millwall, I had made it to and survived the wedding and I was surviving the settling down process. My team however had not survived the third division and was now in Division Four, the lowest of the low. Our now ex-chairman had appointed Martin Peters as a manager on the strength of an illustrious playing career and, just as others had found before, we had found that a World Cup winners medal meant nothing in the world of football management.

The upside was that as a result of our relegation we had a new chairman, a new manager in Ian Porterfield and enough money invested in players to almost guarantee us being the champions before a ball was kicked. This also meant that the away games were to become a bit of a carnival, with our supporters outnumbering the home supporters at most of the grounds.

Now that I was married I had been granted permission to do the away games, as long as I came back the same day, but my financial position had only slightly improved so I needed to find a way to finance the away trips if they were to be reinstated. Then I had an idea. I had been plagued with requests from second raters to come along on our by now infamous away days for a while but I had always turned them down, mainly because I didn't fancy getting stuck in a ruck with a bunch of lightweights, but now it started to look more attractive. I figured I could rent a van and charge enough to make a profit, and it also meant that I would have to tone down the naughty side of the trips if I was with a bunch of wankers. No offence lads.

As I saw it I could get to see most away matches without it costing me a penny. I could save for all the luxuries my wife was suddenly seeing as essential for our new house and I could ease out of the downward spiral towards a life in the underworld without having to suddenly drop it altogether. It was like a drug and I knew I needed to come off slowly if I didn't want to spend the next few years all screwed up and blaming those around me for any twinges of regret I might feel as my life inevitably became more mundane.

I was surprised how easily the rest of the crew accepted the change in the arrangements for away games. While we were going to be seeing as many if not more away games than ever, most would be straight there and straight back after the game with much less of the action that we had all clamoured for in previous seasons. I suppose it couldn't go on forever and I suspect that one or two others were relieved to be calming it down a bit, both from avoiding the inevitable beating we were going to come across on occasions and also from the financial point of view. The weekend trips could cost a bloody fortune and we were all coming across other things we could find to spend our money on.

We still got plenty of scuffles inside the grounds but it all became a bit too easy due to the vast following that we were now taking everywhere. It's funny how the lowest standard we'd played at attracted the biggest support but I suppose that was down to the fact that we were winning most of the time and what a fan really wants to see is his team win.

The van rental thing turned out to be more of a success than I could ever have imagined and I had scores of youths begging for places on trips. Right from the start the pounds rolled in. I had budgeted for ten people on a trip and worked out a price to cover van hire, fuel and my entry to the match. I figured that if I then let the odd extra one squeeze in I would also cover any expenses I might run up for food and drink.

For the first three trips I had between seventeen and twenty passengers all squeezed into the back of a VW van and for the fourth, a trip to York, thirty five were crushed in for what still stands as some sort of record. I don't know how we managed to get the doors shut and I remember thinking if we had come across anything like a hill they would have all had to get out and push. As it was, only twenty two came back as I got a pull from a copper on a push bike who had taken offence to something someone had shouted out of the back of the van as we passed him and had pedalled like fuck to catch us at the next set of traffic lights. Luckily I got off with just a word from the wheezing copper, who looked like he was about to have a heart attack following his exertions, as before he could arrange to have the van weighed and do me for overloading someone sprung open the back doors and most of the thirty five passengers scattered across York leaving the copper with nothing to weigh. He still had a go at me about being responsible for my passengers and keeping them under control.

"I don't like being called a pig on a bike by some thirty five year old drunken idiot." he said aiming his comment at a lad called Paul who had stayed in the van.

"I'm not fucking thirty five." replied Paul, more offended by the coppers estimate of his age than the fact that he had been called a drunken idiot. I later collected as many as I could find from the nearest pub and the rest managed to find their way back by other means.

The match after that was Port Vale. Who the fuck knows where Port Vale is? It's not a fucking place is it? Someone told me it was near Stoke so we headed for Stoke and when we got there Jimmy beckoned a young lad over to the van and then grabbed him and threw him inside. We only let him go after he had directed us to the ground which fortunately for him was only about half a mile from where we kidnapped him.

On the journey to this match everyone actually did have to get out of the van and push as there was no way it was going to make it up Winnats Pass in Castleton, the hill was just too steep. Vans aren't what they used to be. Once there, we gained entry to the main stand at Port Vale by climbing over an advertising hoarding attached to the side of the ground. It had horizontal laths and may as well have been a ladder. It was a piece of piss to climb and saved on the entry money.

We sat in the stand and had a slight altercation with a few Stoke fans who had come along for a bit of action, Stoke had a decent crew and were always good for a scuffle. Then we watched one of our lads, who was being escorted off their kop, stand at the wall at the front of the kop trading blows with Port Vale fans while the coppers escorting him stood and watched.

On the way home I passed a group of Stoke fans who were waiting to ambush our coaches and someone in the back of the van reached over the passenger seat and threw something out of the window trying to hit the mob. Unfortunately it only hit the wing mirror and broke it. In an attempt to avoid losing the deposit on the van we stopped at a car dealer and stole a replacement mirror off a similar vehicle. Back home I attempted to fit the stolen mirror before returning the van and broke the new one as well so I still lost my £20 deposit. Clumsy twat!

Another trip took us to Northampton for a night match. For this game I went in my car. Two hours down the motorway and straight into a pub at the side of the ground. What a pleasant surprise we got when we found out that the fire exit door led straight onto their kop. Five of us sneaked through and then stood directly behind their goal waiting for a crew that never came. After winning 2-1 we went back to the car where we were confronted by around twenty handy looking youths, who could not have been to the game, and we had them on their toes after a scuffle in which Jimmy had ripped the aerial off a van and whipped a black youth with it as he ran away.

"He'll have to go to the clap clinic now." said Jimmy.

Someone fell for it and asked why.

"Because he's got Van Aerial disease." came the predictable reply.

Anyway these and other such trips managed to finance my football habit, provide one or two household goods, keeping the missus sweet, and leave me with a little stash for one of the big events of the year, a trip to Arsenal. We had drawn the Gooners in the League Cup which was to be played over two legs. Fuck knows how but we actually beat the bastards in the first leg. They were in the first division and we were in the fourth and we fucking beat them 1-0. Yes!! The second leg was at Highbury and wild fucking horses would not have kept me away. We arranged to go on the football special train which British Rail were running and met up in the Howard Hotel across from the station. After playing pool and nicking a few of the balls we got on the train and made it to London without incident.

There were a good few of us and the coppers marched us towards the ground. As we approached Highbury we were confronted by a large mob of Arsenal lads who gave us some verbals but it was clear they hadn't really taken us seriously, us being in the fourth division and all. Boy did they get a shock when we broke through the police lines and gave it to them right on their own doorstep. To be fair they stood and fought and neither side backed off until the coppers restored order.

Inside the ground the atmosphere was tense and the match was quite tight but in the end we lost two-nil to go out by the odd goal. We played well but just couldn't manage to sneak the away goal that would have taken us through. The real highlight for me though was when, after some goading, a skinny kid we called Narrowback threw one of the stolen pool balls towards an angry mob of Arsenal lads who were stood on the side terrace near to where we were stood on the clock end. The ball hit one of their mob smack on the head and bounced onto the pitch. Instead of celebrating the shot Narrowback went white and threw up on the terrace. Soft twat!

Anyway after the game we got back to the train and thought we had made it safely away only to get a rude awakening when the train was ambushed by Arsenal bastards at Potters Bar who bombarded the train with bricks breaking several windows and leaving us to complete the journey with slightly more ventilation than when we started.

Chapter 14

COWBOYS AND CATERPILLARS

Torquay Utd 1 – 1 Blades
14th November 1981

While the drop to the fourth division had been a blow it did have the benefit of making us the biggest fish in a small pond. Being the top of any division does give you some pride back. It also had the benefit of placing us in the same division as Torquay United. What a gig, Torquay away, even newly married, semi-retired, sort of rehabilitating hooligans had to give this one a go. So the van was booked, the wife was sweet talked and bribed into giving permission to go for the weekend and a crew was lined up for the big event.

Most of the old faces were still around (except Stacey) and there were a few new lads lined up for the trip who were handy without been reckless and apparently good for a laugh. These lads were not to be relied on in a big battle but were guaranteed to do something daft and have you in stitches laughing. The emphasis on this trip was to have a good time, Torquay didn't figure in hooligan terms and no trouble was expected. We were heading for seaside, beer and a fun weekend away with the lads. That's what I had told the wife and for once that was exactly what I intended to do.

We had arranged to set off on Friday night, rough it on the way down and get lodgings in a guesthouse for Saturday night in Torquay then come back Sunday with a lunch stop en-route. We met in a pub in the town centre around five-o clock and by half past I had counted everyone on board collected the fares and set off down the M1. The plan was to get as far as we could by eight and then have a session wherever we were, sleep at motorway services and make Torquay for breakfast.

At eight-o clock we were at Tewkesbury. None of us had ever been there before but as we were not looking for trouble and we had never heard of the place it seemed as good as anywhere. We pulled into a car park near what was billed as the town centre and got out for a scout around. After ten minutes the scouting was done. There's not much to see in Tewkesbury.

We had established that there were just a handful of pubs and as far as we could make out just the one club which was around the back of one of the pubs, so to make it easier on the legs that was the pub we settled in. The early evening passed without anything worthy of note other than that we found out one of the new lads was a bit of a kleptomaniac. He stole things without realising it at times and it was mostly stuff that was of no real use to anyone. We had only stopped for a piss at services on the way down and he had a cup and saucer and a roll of hand towel from the gents in the back of the van. Jimmy christened him Fingers.

We found out that the club at the rear of the pub was free entry before 10.30 and also that they didn't admit large groups of lads so at ten-o clock we started drifting round to the club in pairs arranging to meet up inside by half past. Jimmy and me were second to go and we arrived at the club to find it was like something out of an old gangster movie. We had to first knock on the door then a small hatch opened up and a pair of mean looking eyes gave us the once over before the door was unbolted to let us in. Then, somewhat disconcertingly, the door was bolted up again behind us. I don't know how that fits in with the fire regulations but it didn't sit comfortably with my *'how do I get out in a hurry if it all goes tits up'* regulations.

Once inside we had a good look around to get our bearings. The place turned out to be quite good. It was a bit like the Crazy Daisy with low, vaulted ceilings and several small booths with tables and benches set out for groups of eight. It was an L shaped place with one leg of the L taken up by the booth seating arrangement and the other leg making up the dance floor area. The bar was in the bottom corner of the L with a good view of both areas, Toilets were in the bit behind the angle of the L and there was an emergency exit at the far end of the dance floor. There was seating for around 100 people in the booth area and there were additional tables and stools scattered around the perimeter of the dance floor.

When we got in the seats were about half full and there were just two girls dancing, but by the time we had got our drinks in (coke for me with the drive ahead) the place was beginning to fill up. We took our seats in one of the booths with Fingers and a lad called Dave who had very narrow eyes and a pock marked face and as far as I could recall hadn't said a word all night. One of his already narrow eyes was closed due to a black eye he had picked up in the week so Jimmy had christened him One Lamp Louie on the spot. Jimmy was going through a phase of giving people nicknames at the time. After a few minutes we were joined by the rest of our crew, ten in total, and we all crammed around the one booth. We drank and chatted for about an hour and it wasn't until I had to visit the toilets that I noticed the locals starting to gather around us. We hadn't figured on any opposition as this was not football country and being totally into football we were oblivious to anything else. Coming back from the toilets, and being totally sober in a club full of people well on the way to being drunk I was able to see things from a different perspective. I paused and looked at our crew in the booth. They were by now well on the way and were getting quite rowdy though not aggressive. The locals having spotted strange faces and heard our northern accents were watching closely and had begun to gather around us. They were not football fans like us so from that point of view there was no immediate rivalry, but they were young men faced with a group of outsiders on their turf and human nature said that sooner or later something would kick off. It also appeared that most of the locals were members of the same rugby club and built like brick shithouses.

As I was pondering what to do next and thinking how we could get out of the booth and into an area we could more easily defend ourselves or escape from if it kicked off, I felt a tap on my shoulder. I turned around expecting it to be a challenge from some egg-chasing bumpkin but instead found myself faced by a rather attractive barmaid. Before I could start to think whether I was being propositioned or not (not that I would have been interested, being a married man and all that!) she told me that the manager would like a word.

I went over to the end of the bar where the manager was waiting and, rather than being ejected which is what I was expecting, the manager asked if my friends had a favourite drink. Somewhat taken aback I said that most of them liked a drop of Guinness. The manager then said that if I could persuade my lot to leave by the back door he would give us a crate of Guinness to see us on our way. I couldn't believe it, I was thinking of trying to get them out before anything started anyway and the manager offers to throw some booze in as well. I went back over to the booth and spoke to Jimmy and Fingers and we decided to take up the manager's offer. So we all left via the back of the bar and out through the yard that was shared by the pub and the club. Jimmy collected the Guinness and we all made our way back to the van ready to move on further south and to find a motorway services for a sleep.

As we were loading the van with the Guinness, and the crate of cider that Fingers had somehow managed to lift from the club, we were suddenly confronted by the sound of gunfire and running footsteps. We looked into the street and saw a man being chased by about fifteen others who appeared to be shooting at him. The man ran onto the car park and stopped about twenty yards from the van. We were all stood on the other side of the van which was parked in a dark unlit corner of the car park out of sight of the armed mob. Jimmy quietly handed out a few bottles and a brush stale that Fingers had nicked from the pub we met in back home. I whispered to Jimmy

"What are we supposed to do with bottles and a brush against a gang armed with guns?"

"I'm going to hit as many as I can before they shoot me." said Jimmy. Then before I had chance to call him a daft twat he was off at them screaming like some madman which I was beginning to think was exactly what he was.

Without any more thought and because I wasn't about to let a mate down, despite my reservations about the sanity of what he was doing, I also rushed at the gunmen and was amazed to find the rest of our crew followed me. Not one of them bottled it. The gang of 'gunmen' shit themselves and scattered all over Tewkesbury in the face of our assault leaving behind their original target who, after getting over the shock of us appearing yelling and screaming out of the darkness told us what was going on. It turned out he was a member of a cowboy society who once a month had a meeting where they all dressed up in their outfits and acted out scenes from cowboy films. This month they were doing one where he got rounded up and ran out of town. Only our interference had altered the script somewhat. We left him still a little perturbed and set off for the Bristol area laughing at the night's events and wondering what would have happened if the guns had been real.

I pulled into a service station on the M5 at the bottom edge of Bristol at about 1.15 in the morning and we all went inside for something to eat and hopefully to find somewhere warmer and more comfortable than the van to get a bit of sleep. There were three people serving and about a dozen people, mostly lorry drivers sat about eating and drinking. Fingers walked up to the counter and loaded his plate up with food and then ate it as he moved slowly towards the till. It seemed that everyone in the place had seen him except the woman on the till. He finished the last of the food just as she was serving the bloke in front of him and coolly paid for the cup of tea which was the only thing left on his tray. I took the more conventional route and paid for a cheese and tomato sandwich and a cup of coffee.

After we had eaten we decided to split up and find somewhere to get our heads down as we expected to get moved on if all ten of us were hanging around together for any length of time. I found a quiet corner and, using a few chairs as a screen to keep out of sight, laid on the floor under a table and tried to get what sleep I could.

We had arranged to meet back at the van at 5am and after about three hours fitful sleep I made my way back. Jimmy arrived at the van at the same time as me. He told me he had slept on a bench in a corridor and when he woke up there were a handful of coins beside him. People must have taken him for homeless which was an easy mistake to make, Jimmy wasn't the best-dressed bloke I knew. Dave was back at the van already; he had slept in the toilets and had come back to the van early after apparently being propositioned by a shifty looking bloke in a pink shirt. All the others except Fingers had slept in the van having found no suitable alternative or having been moved on by service station staff.

We sat and waited for Fingers who turned up at ten past five carrying a cardboard box filled with cleaning materials and toilet rolls. He told us that he had slept in a cleaner's cupboard and had become attached to the stuff. God knows why he wanted it. I would have thought he would have used his condition to collect things of more value but what do I know. Anyway we loaded Fingers and his stuff into the van and set off for Torquay.

We Arrived in Torquay in darkness at about half past six in the morning and pulled up right at the side of the harbour. About half an hour later two more vans pulled up alongside and we greeted the occupants with a cheer as we recognised them as fellow fans. Jimmy

160

and me got out and spoke to some of the lads in the other vans. They told us they had spent the evening in Sheffield and then driven down overnight and were going to get some sleep before anywhere opened up. A gang of lads who were well known for their cannabis smoking habit occupied one of the vans. It was obvious from the smoke filled interior of the van and the spaced out expressions on the faces of the passengers that they had been on the weed all the way down. God knows how the driver made it, as he must have been out of his skull from the smoke without having to do a joint of his own.

A skinhead who, due to his diminutive stature, was known as Jockey occupied the passenger seat. He was laid across the double front seat in a green sleeping bag with his arms tucked inside and only his head showing. He had wound down the window and lay with his head protruding from the van presumably to get access to some oxygen as there was very little inside the van.

In the other van were a group of lads who we saw at most away games. One of them was Giddy Bill. He was a bit of a stroke puller and had been in trouble several times for daft tricks. He once had half the Cambridge police force trying to get him down from a floodlight pylon and had on another occasion been caught trying to have it away with Hull City's entire team kit.

We stood talking for a bit until the rising sun started to illuminate a little more detail of our surroundings. Giddy Bill had been glancing around the harbour and having spotted something he liked the look of said he'd see us later and wandered off. Jimmy informed me, quite unnecessarily, that he was 'busting for a shit' and having grabbed a couple of boxes of service station toilet paper from the back of the van he wandered off down an alley between two shops.

Fingers then turned up with a crate of milk that he had '*found*' and distributed his swag to the gathering throng, most of whom drank the milk and threw the empties into the edge of the harbour.

Two or three more vans had arrived at the harbour side and quite a crowd was building up. There was a small cheer and a bit of laughing as some of the lads spotted Giddy Bill who had managed to free a small rowing boat from its moorings and propel it, with himself on board into the middle of the harbour. As he had forgotten

161

to steal any oars he was now splashing away trying to propel himself back with his hands and getting nowhere fast.

I was just starting to wonder how long it would be before something went pear shaped or we were joined by the boys in blue when I got the answer to both. The relative quiet was suddenly broken by a metallic banging sound and shouting coming from the alley where Jimmy had gone. The next moment Jimmy came running out of the alley holding his trousers somewhere around his knees and leaving a trail of toilet paper behind him. He was followed by a Chinese man waving a stick and calling him a dirty bastard. Jimmy jumped into the back of the first van he came to which happened to be the ganja van. Not being one to waste an opportunity to get high he did not re-appear for some time.

At this point the first police car arrived. A fat red-faced copper got out of the car and put on his hat. Rather than wading in and arresting everyone in sight, as was normally the case, he simply walked slowly over to the side of the harbour near where we were assembled. He then stood looking out to sea, with the flotilla of bobbing milk bottles masked by the overhanging harbour edge and Giddy Bill splashing frantically away just out of his vision, and said loudly, but to no one in particular, in a slow drawling west country accent.

"Lovely place Torbay, be a shame to spoil it."

"Shut up you Welsh bastard." shouted Jockey who was still laid in his sleeping bag with his head out of the window.

That's done it I thought but the copper, cool as a cucumber, walked slowly over to Jockey, tipped his hat back slightly and with his head tilted to one side said to Jockey in the same slow drawl "And who do you think you are?"

Jockey, obviously high on the weed, started wriggling around in his green sleeping bag, his arms still by his side and shouted "I'm a fucking caterpillar, who the fuck are you?"

The whole assembled mob were pissing themselves laughing as the copper who still rates as one of the coolest I have ever come across took hold of Jockeys sleeping bag and pulled it, with Jockey stuck inside, straight out of the van window and deposited him on the tarmac. As two other coppers picked Jockey up to carry him away the cool cop said "Well boy when you turn into a butterfly I might think about releasing you."

He then returned to the side of the harbour and, still talking to no one in particular, said "Right then once you lot have picked up all that paper you've dropped you can be on your way out of my harbour, and I'm sure you won't need to come back."

Then, still having not once looked in the direction of Giddy Bill, he added "And will someone please get that fool off of the water before he drowns himself."

Then without further ado he got back into his car and drove away. Incredibly most of the mob started picking up the litter and putting it into litter bins, we then got back into our vans and left the harbour.

There had been a loose arrangement among our travelling fans that we would meet at the big green behind the beach about eleven-o clock. So we spent the morning finding a café and having breakfast and then searching for lodgings. After been turned away from several hotels all claiming that they were full, despite Torquay having virtually closed for the winter, we eventually found a guest house, at the top of a bloody great hill in Babbacombe, that was prepared to take all ten of us in, but not before the landlady had taken the money in advance, the van registration and the details from my driving license.

We left the van at the lodgings and walked down into Torquay, which by that time was starting to fill up with our fans who were determined to make an occasion of it. By eleven-o clock a stranger would have sworn it was still summer season as the front was crawling with people. Our fans were on the beach, on the promenade and outside every bar. The green where we were due to meet up was covered with our lot and someone had produced a football and started a game, which we joined in. After about ten minutes there must have been over one hundred a side and it was bedlam. The pitch had grown from its original size of about fifty yards by twenty and now included the whole green. If the ball was on grass it was in play. There were now no goals and the point of the game seemed to be for any individual to try to get to the ball and kick it as far as they could. The whole two hundred would then rush towards the ball and kick it away again. It was like football returning to its roots (or watching the pigs).

One lad tried to pick the ball up and was jumped on by about twenty others, punching and kicking at him. The ball came out after a few seconds but the punch up lasted about five minutes as the game went on around it. Then one lad tried a slide tackle and got up covered in dog shit and mud which slowed the game down a little as everyone suddenly started looking more carefully where they were going. It eventually ended when someone kicked the ball onto the road and it burst as it was run over by a lorry.

Our exercise had made us thirsty so we set off to find a pub and throughout the early afternoon we gradually made our way, via various pubs, back up the hill to Babbacombe and Torquay United's ground, which turned out to be about one hundred yards from our digs. There had not been one incident of real trouble all day and the police had kept to the background, occasionally moving a group on if they were getting a bit rowdy but in a friendly way. If only all police were like that there might not be half the trouble there was.

We got to the ground and the game took its usual course. Torquay put ten men behind the ball and tried to stifle our game, which was the usual tactic against us that season. To be fair it was the only way as we were playing in the fourth Division but had recruited good second division standard players. We were the big fish in a small pond and we were playing probably the best football since our glory days in the top flight. The results of that season proved the point as we were to take the Division Four title with what was then a record points haul and we lost only four games all season. Torquay had done their homework and worked hard and in the end got a one all draw which for them was a victory and for us was slightly disappointing but still acceptable.

As was the case at most games that season our support vastly outnumbered the home support and so there were no confrontations outside the ground as the Torquay fans scurried off back to their homes, (who would want hassle if they lived here anyway).

A good number of our fans were staying the night and there was talk of meeting up by the harbour for a pub-crawl before doing a club later on. In the end we decided to leave them to it and stay up at

Babbacombe for the night. It was probably the thought of getting back up that bloody hill that did it, so, reasonably happy with the result we went back to our digs to get changed for the evening session.

Before we went out we checked the results on TV. We found out that the Pigs, who had played QPR that day, had lost 3-1 which lifted our spirits no end. I suppose it's a bit sad really, but because of the fierce rivalry between the Blades and the Pigs, each set of supporters seems to take more pleasure in seeing their rivals lose than seeing their own team win. When you've had as many Monday mornings getting an earful from a bunch of Pig morons as I have over the years you may start to understand. If the other lot has lost they tend to shut up to avoid getting a bit back. The trouble with the Pigs is that while at that time they could only draw an attendance around the same level as us, they seemed to have around 100,000 more '*supporters*' who never go to games but claim allegiance if it means they can have a go at us. So the Pigs losing was an important part of our weekend.

Anyway buoyed by news of their defeat we set off for the pubs of Babbacombe and after about an hour, and three deserted pubs we were beginning to wonder if we would have been better going into Torquay after all. The only other face we had seen, apart from bar staff, was a young Scottish lad who had come down to Torquay to find work in the summer and was now spending a lonely winter unemployed and a long way from home. For some reason he had struck up a quick friendship with Fingers. If he was hoping to bum a few drinks of him he had definitely picked the wrong one. I felt like warning him but he came across as a bit of a sad twat so I left Fingers to it, wondering what the Scot could possibly have that would be worth stealing.

I spoke to Jimmy and we were on the point of rounding everyone up to head for Torquay when there was a sudden burst of female laughter from the room at the other side of the pub. If Jimmy had been a dog you would have seen his ears prick up and his tail start wagging, as it is it only seemed like that. Without a word Jimmy was off to the other room, hunting down the source of the laughter. The rest of us followed at a pace less likely to break our necks and found Jimmy already into it.

165

At first glance I thought 'typical Jimmy fodder'. He was stood next to a fat bird that looked for all the world just like Alison Moyet. I don't mean similar I am talking spitting images here. A very plain looking girl who, to my eyes, appeared to be about twelve years old accompanied the fat bird. She must have been older because she was drinking spirits and anyone who looked that young must have been asked for proof of age by the barman. The fat bird was drinking a fucking great cocktail with sparklers and umbrellas sticking out. If it hadn't been for the foot long straw she would have poked her eye out trying to drink it.

There were no other people in the bar and I was just thinking about making my excuses to Jimmy, who knowing him would be hanging around these two birds until he got a shag or a slap, and heading for Torquay when the fat bird asked what everyone was drinking. None of us wanted to offend the girl by refusing so we rushed the bar and ordered our drinks before she had the chance to change her mind or do the arithmetic. Minutes later, when we had downed our drinks, the fat one shouted "Same again." and we replenished our drinks at the bar for free once more.

I decided to take a closer look at this bird so I joined Jimmy and gave her the once over. Once I had focused my eyes on the person rather than the fat then it became a bit clearer. Heavy gold jewellery hung from her wrists and neck, both hands were adorned by good quality rings and on closer inspection her clothes, hair and make-up were of a quality not usually seen on the type of girl we associated with. Clearly this girl had money.

Jimmy invited me to take a seat and introduced me to the girls but not visa versa. I presumed Jimmy had not got around to asking names yet. He usually left that sort of detail until the after sex dialogue. The fat bird then opened a small enamelled box, which she had produced from her handbag and offered us a pick of the contents. There were half a dozen small white pills inside and Jimmy selected one and with no hesitation put it in his mouth and swallowed it, washed down with a gulp of whisky. I, being a little less reckless than Jimmy, selected a pill, palmed it and pretended to take it. Even if I could have been sure of what it was I wouldn't have taken it. In my view drugs are the one sure way to oblivion. I was even steady

166

with the drink, usually drinking shandy while the others had beer. I liked to be in reasonable control, especially when away from home. The few scrapes where we had come out worst had all been when we were all too drunk to realise what was happening soon enough and that was evidence enough to keep my intoxicant intake down. Sad Scottish wankers on the other hand could have as many drugs as they wanted. So I dropped my pill into his drink while he was talking bollocks to Fingers.

I left Jimmy and wandered around the boys chatting about the days events and our drinks were topped up at regular intervals on the fat birds tab. I changed my order to just Coke after the third round. I had a long drive home the next day and by the way the others were knocking it back I figured they might need a bit of guidance later. Fortunately we were in a sedate seaside town and not some big city where a bunch of pissed up northern boys would have been a soft target for any crew wanting some easy action. Nevertheless I preferred the better safe than sorry approach so I stayed pretty much sober. The others were well pissed and happy with it and when the fat bird suggested having a party at her place there was unanimous agreement.

Fingers had been talking to the sad Scot all night and at the mention of a party Fingers volunteered the Scot to provide the music. I wondered why he presumed a bird with as much apparent wealth as the fat bird was displaying might need some lonely down and out to lend her some records but I presumed Fingers had a motive. So Fingers and the Scot set off to collect the music. Everyone else headed for the street.

As we all piled out of the pub Jimmy stumbled and fell to the floor. Partly to show off and partly to hide his embarrassment Jimmy started to do press-ups. To everyone's surprise, as Jimmy got up, the fat bird said "I can do that," and dropped to the floor to demonstrate. What she couldn't do, due to a mixture of excess weight and the drink/drug mix in her stomach, was to get back up off the floor. She had two attempts before rolling over on her back, laughing loudly and waving her legs in the air like a dying fly. Jimmy, taking it as an invitation, dropped on top of her and started simulating sex. The fat bird clamped her legs around him and said "I hope you can get it up for real when we get to my place."

I tried to picture the scene and felt ill. Jimmy on the other hand said "Result", jumped up and pulled the fat bird to her feet. She then amazed us all by producing a set of car keys, opening the door of a BMW parked across the road and driving off with Jimmy in the passenger seat grinning like a Cheshire cat. The other bird said she'd show the rest of us the way to the flat and, as Fingers and the Scot arrived with a pile of LPs, we all set off up the road. I had decided that I was not going to the party, I'd promised the wife that I'd behave and for all my faults I always keep a promise, and feeling pretty sure the rest of the crew would be OK I split from the bunch and went back to the digs to watch Match of the Day.

It was about 2.30 am when the first of them arrived back at the digs. Fingers, One Lamp and the lad known as Narrowback due to his skinny stature were the first. They were like the Three Kings at Christmas. Several LPs, origin Scotland, a lava lamp ex fat bird and a traffic cone courtesy of Torbay District Council were their gifts; Fingers strikes again! Everyone else trickled back over the next half hour and when Jimmy arrived at 3 am with a neck looking like a victim of the Boston Strangler we were all present and correct and ready for some shut eye.

Next morning found us assembled at the breakfast table at 9 am in varying states of health, all except Narrowback managed to eat an excellent breakfast served up by the best landlady in the Torquay area. She had tidied up the mess we had left, got us all up at the requested time of eight o clock, never mentioned the mess or noise and even thrown in a packed lunch for our journey home; priceless.

We eventually set off for home just after ten o clock. It was a long drive and the plan was to stop somewhere about half way for a drink and some lunch and then get home for tea. Jimmy rode shotgun and Narrowback, who was still feeling a bit queasy took the seat between Jimmy and me. The lads were all talking about the party the previous night and about the fat birds flat. Apparently it was well posh. State of the art everything; god knows what she did for a living. Maybe she was Alison Moyet!

The roads were quiet and it wasn't long before we were passing Exeter. There was a slip road coming onto the motorway and as I passed it I noticed a girl on the hard shoulder just at the bottom of the slip road. She had her thumb out gesturing for a lift. Jimmy also spotted her and told me to pull over. I pulled up about fifty yards past the girl and glanced in the near side mirror. I could see the girl running towards the van carrying a rucksack. I expected her to take one look at this van full of horny young men and run the whole fifty yards back. When she reached the van I noticed just how attractive she was, she stood about five foot six in her trainers. She had dark hair, shoulder length, which framed her tanned face which was just on the healthy side of thin (I can't be doing with anorexic types) and had a look that I associated with something but could not quite put my finger on. She had an athletic build and when she was running towards the van I could notice, even in the mirror that she had bumps where bumps should be. Then again I would notice that!

Jimmy wound down the window of the van and as she spoke I realised what the look was. She said in a very thick French accent "Manchester; you go to Manchester yes?"

"Sure," said Jimmy "we're going to Manchester, jump in."

No way, I thought, but to my surprise she asked Jimmy to open the back doors. Jimmy was having none of that and he bundled Narrowback over the double passenger seat into the back of the van and opened the door to let the girl in. Jimmy got out and took the girls bag which he threw into the back the same way Narrowback had just gone. Fingers eyes lit up but Jimmy gave him the sort of stare that that makes guard dogs cower in fright and Fingers got the message. The girl took the seat vacated by Narrowback and Jimmy got in beside her. Jimmy asked her name and she replied with something none of us could get our tongues around so Jimmy said we would call her 'Jacque a Paul'. Fuck knows where he got that one from but she didn't seem to mind and said "You English, you are crazee bananas".

Jimmy did an impression of her French accent which seemed to amuse her and then began to question her about her origins, where she was going etc. It turns out that she was French (surprise!) and she was backpacking around Europe in a year out from university. It also

169

turned out that she had been raped while hitchhiking through Hungary yet she still got in a van full of young English hooligans. She must love it. Jimmy also found out that while her English was better than his French, she only understood the basic text book stuff and could not get to grips with even the most simple slang or colloquial terminology. He was soon winding her up with suggestive remarks which she had no idea of the meaning, much to the amusement of the lads in the back. He also confused her with his Yorkshire accent, which he tried to teach her with mixed results. By the time we reached Droitwitch, our planned lunch time stop, he had got her saying *'Ey up flower'*, in a passable accent and unknowingly admitting to having had anal sex with three dwarfs due to Jimmy's mixture of double entendre and slang expressions in his questioning. She just sat there smiling and nodding, Poor girl.

It was about twelve thirty when we pulled up outside a pub on the outskirts of Droitwitch and we all piled in and ordered food and drinks and settled down for a session. Jimmy treated 'Jacque a Paul' to a traditional Sunday lunch and a pint of Guinness which she accepted with gratitude in the case of the food and disbelief on tasting the Guinness for the first time. Jimmy explained that it was an acquired taste, which meant nothing to her so he bought her a white wine and at some point shortly afterwards they sloped off to the back of the van. Not so 'Crazy Bananas' if you ask me.

At two o clock the barman called time so we all went back to the van. Jimmy and his European friend had finished whatever it was they had been doing and were giving each other language lessons, which continued as I drove up the motorway. Jacque a Paul could now say *'Shut thi gob'* quite expertly and Jimmy was stuck on 'Crazee Bananas' with a slight accent. I suppose if he had wanted to learn French he would have gone to school, which he hadn't very often. At least the talk had taken the girls eye off the road signs which were now saying anything but Manchester.

The rest of the lads had fallen asleep in the back of the van and I was having a job staying awake myself but eventually we made it back home. I pulled up outside Sheffield railway station and Jimmy who had just woken up and realised where we were let Jacque a Paul out. As she got out of the van she said in her lovely French accent "You have taken me to Manchester, Yes?"

'"No but there's a train in there that will." said Jimmy getting back into the van. I drove off to the sound of French obscenities being shouted at the van and then dropped the rest of the lads off before returning home for some well-earned sleep.

Chapter 15

MONKEY HANGERS AND FAT MINGERS

Scunthorpe Utd 2 – 1 Blades
20th February 1982

Hartlepool 2 – 3 Blades
6th March 1982

I hadn't particularly planned it as such but Torquay turned out to be the last weekender we did. I was settling down to married life and now I had my own home I enjoyed going back to it. The craving for kicks had faded some time ago and while I had enjoyed the last few trips, I had found myself looking forward to getting home virtually as soon as I had set off. That didn't mean I stopped going to football. My team was enjoying the most successful season in its history even if it was in the fourth division. We were winning, we were taking a bigger following to away matches than we had ever done and every match was like a carnival.

At most grounds we outnumbered the home support by at least two to one and other than a little token resistance there was not much trouble to speak of, although every now and again we did come across a bit of action. Sometimes it was in unexpected areas and usually it was a home crew reinforced by 'guests' from more illustrious neighbouring towns. Sometimes it was just game locals lads defending their turf and one time it was a monster of a bird showing the wimp locals how it was done.

The most notable exchange was probably Hartlepool, the monkey hangers. For anyone who doesn't know, the natives of Hartlepool are known as monkey hangers because legend says that during the Napoleonic war a monkey was washed up from a shipwreck in the North Sea. The local peasants, having never seen either a monkey or a Frenchman before, mistook it for a French spy and hung it by the neck 'til it were dead. Nice people but not too bright. They were a game set but they would probably not have bothered if it weren't for significant reinforcements from Sunderland who had heard of our growing reputation and had come to have a pop.

I had stopped doing the vans after losing my deposit yet again when some cowardly fans had vandalised our van while we were inside the ground at Altringham in a cup replay which to my shame we lost 3-0. It was the first time I had actually lost money on a trip and I wasn't going to lose any more. So I went to Hartlepool in my car. Jimmy, Dick and Dick's younger brother Keith were the passengers and after stopping somewhere in the sticks on the way up we arrived in Hartlepool about one o-clock.

As we drove through town we could see that it had already kicked off. There was a large pub in a shopping centre and outside were about two hundred of our lot and about fifty coppers, some with dogs. As we passed closer we could see the footpath covered with broken glass and the pub had several windows smashed. We decided to give the town a miss as there was too much police activity and it looked like it was too late as there were no Hartlepool fans to be seen, so having found the ground and parked up, we blagged our way into a working men's club behind the ground. The locals were friendly, the beer was cheap and we played snooker until 2.45. It was all very civilised, no trouble, no worries.

We had been playing snooker with a couple of monkey hangers and when it was time to go to the match they joined us. A couple of times in the past we had gone to games and stood on the side terracing with the locals and enjoyed a bit of banter without trouble kicking off. At Hartlepool we decided we would do the same. To be honest it was getting a bit boring chasing bunches of fourth division limp dicks off broken down kops. Hartlepool turned out to be different.

We went into the ground and found ourselves on a side terrace in front of what was their main stand. As we faced the pitch the kop was to our right and most of our fans were behind the goal to our left or on the opposite side terrace. There were also a few faces I recognised in the stand behind us. Probably about thirty decent lads, all fighters all sat quietly sussing out the opposition before making themselves known.

At most grounds the side terracing was separated from the area behind the goals by fencing or walls and clubs charged extra for a view from the side of the pitch, but at Hartlepool there was no barrier and you could walk freely between the kop and the terrace. While the intention had been having a bit of harmless banter, the proximity and ease of access to their crew proved irresistible. I suggested to Jimmy that we had a wander onto the kop to find out how good the monkey hangers were. Jimmy and Dick were keen and Keith said he would give it a go but he was a bit nervous. Keith was a couple of years younger than us and had only just started going to away matches.

We wandered over to the kop and stood directly behind the goal. Hartlepool had a crew of about one hundred and I figured that about twenty would be any good and the rest were just makeweights. Nevertheless twenty, plus eighty back up, onto three and a half was a bit too high odds on uncharted territory. I had a look around to see if there were any more of our lot on the kop. Sometimes there would be four or five separate groups infiltrating an away end and they would all merge together for an assault. This time I could spot none of the usual suspects. Some we had already seen in the stand and others must have failed in their attempts to evade the police spotters who manned the turnstiles looking for away fans. Not fancying the odds as they were we decided to go back to the terrace for a bit while we could get maybe half a dozen reinforcements to go back and have a pop. So we started to head back to the terrace.

The trouble was we had been spotted and a group of four monkey hangers stood in the path at the front of the kop. One took up the pose and was bouncing around in front of us while the others looked on. I figured I could probably take the four on my own, they were amateurs. If they had been the business they would have just waded in and given us a kicking. I stepped forward from our group towards the bouncing one and said in my best John Wayne voice "Make your move boy!"

It was as I thought, they were wankers and the bouncing one stopped bouncing and backed off into his group of shit soft friends who in turn backed off a couple of steps. Grasping the opportunity while they were on the retreat I lunged forward and swung a boot at the one who had been bouncing knocking him off balance and sending his mates and about twenty onlookers scurrying up the kop leaving a conspicuous hole in the crowd. Fortunately most of the coppers were stood guard over our fans in other parts of the ground so our little altercation went relatively unnoticed and we found ourselves with enough time to melt away into the crowd and back round onto the terrace.

While we had not been noticed by the police we had now made ourselves known to the monkey hangers who, a few at a time started to wind their way over to our position. We took up a stance at the back of the terrace where there was a barrier about four feet high

176

between the terracing and a walkway. Behind the walkway was the main stand where there were now about fifty of our lot sat in a group. This meant that the Hartlepool fans would not come from behind as they ran the risk of being showered in hot drinks or broken seating. So with the advantage of height and a view of everything going on around us we let the monkey hangers build up a crew.

As their crew was building up around us one or two would come over and say something but they hadn't the bottle to wade in so we shared a bit of banter and gave one or two a fuck off tablet if they got too cocky. One in particular was a bit of a knob head and he produced a business card to Jimmy.

"What the fuck is that?" said Jimmy.

"It's to warn you that I do karate." said the knob head

"Well this is to warn you that I wear steel cap boots." said Jimmy as he kicked the lad hard in the shins.

The knob head hobbled back into the crowd which had now built up to around fifty strong and had attracted the attention of our lads in the stand who were giving them some verbals. Some of them had recognised us and knew what would be coming. I gave a wink to the odd one and felt reassured that if it all went pear shaped that there was some backup around.

The game kicked off and most of the monkey hangers had one eye on the game and one eye on us. A couple of their lot tried to get in close but were put off by a few hard stares and harsh words from us and there was a bit of a stand-off. They hadn't got the bottle to wade in and we were wary of the police at pitch side who were keeping an eye on the stand above us. We didn't want ejecting before the game had got warmed up. Then it went tits up. Hartlepool scored on what must have been their first serious attack and the crowd around us went wild. One of their lot stepped towards us shaking both fists in the air in celebration and I mistook it for having a pop. I lashed out with my boot and caught him right in his wedding tackle. Suddenly the whole Hartlepool mob waded in covered by the goal celebrations and the usual mayhem that brings. I was engulfed by around twenty of them but they had got too close so they couldn't really swing at me and what blows I took were doing no damage. The problem was the crowd had closed in so far that I couldn't swing either. Then someone grabbed me by the hair and dragged my head downwards. Suddenly all I could see were feet kicking out towards my face and all I could feel were thumps raining down on my head and back. I couldn't actually feel much pain but I went all claustrophobic and I could hear a ringing in my ears.

The red mist came down and I lost it big style. For onlookers it must have been like watching the incredible hulk as I summoned up all my strength and with one almighty push I straightened up and started lashing out wildly at anyone anywhere near me. I landed quite a lot of glancing blows, which did no damage but created a bit of space. I also landed a couple of real beauties, which sent two monkey hangers sprawling. I had created myself a bit of space and as the Hartlepool mob backed off I made the most of the situation and charged down into them. The others had been on the fringes of the action and on seeing me having a pop joined in and we all kicked and punched our way down to the bottom of the terrace. At the bottom the coppers were jumping into the crowd and I expected to be ejected but to my surprise they just pushed us back into the mob and told us to calm down. I suppose they must have thought the scuffling was just a rowdy goal celebration and they hadn't realised we were away fans.

The Hartlepool fans surrounded us again but stood off a bit now the coppers were among us. Then Jimmy asked me if I had seen Keith. I quickly scanned the crowd and could not see him. Dick did the same and we presumed that he was still deep inside the monkey hangers mob. Not wanting to see Keith get a proper beating so early in his hooligan career I decided to go find him and ran swinging at the mob again. Jimmy and Dick followed and we soon moved the Hartlepool out of the way but still we could not see Keith. Then as the coppers finally got the idea and came swarming around us I heard Keith shout from up in the stand. The cheeky bastard had jumped up into the seats as soon as it first kicked off and had sat looking down from above as we collected bumps and bruises trying to rescue him. The coppers rounded us up and to my amazement escorted us up into the seats with the fifty or so of our lot rather than throwing us out or arresting us. Thanks lads.

We presumed that our escapades were finished for the day but within ten minutes we were proved wrong, as we became aware of an atmosphere building to our left. There was no actual threat or gesture or comment from the block of seats to our left but the mood seemed to change slightly. I scanned the crowd and started to notice one or two faces that didn't fit. You would normally have expected that part of the ground to be full of old blokes or families but there were several lads of our age scattered about and every few minutes another would take his place. The old blokes knew what was going on and before long they started to move one by one until there were just the young ones left. Then all at once the new boys started chanting at us. It turns out they were mostly Sunderland fans who had come to have a pop at us and we obliged by wading in as best we could among the seats. The coppers soon split us up and for the rest of the half there was the odd shouted threat and an occasional scuffle where the line of coppers was weakest.

The action alerted all the other scrappers in the ground and it wasn't long before we were well outnumbered in the stand and the coppers were struggling to keep us apart. Half time was going to be the key and to be fair to the coppers they knew it as well. On the half time whistle we all stood and headed for the back of the stand where the action would take place. The cops were ready and before there was time for any scrapping to begin they quickly surrounded us and herded us down to the pitch side. We were then marched around to the terrace where most of our fans were and we took our place to chants of "Barmy Army, Barmy Army" and we were surrounded by those who hadn't the bottle to go on the home end wanting to know all the details. As usual there were the exaggerated tales of heroics from the ones who had stood as far away from the action as they could get. I soon got fed up and wandered off to watch the second half away from the story tellers.

The second half passed without much incident and the game finished in a three – two victory to the blades and another three points towards our record haul that season. After the game we made our way back to the car and about half a mile into our journey home I screeched to a halt as I caught a glimpse of a flying brick heading for my windscreen. My evasive action was a partial success as the brick landed short of smashing the glass but left me with a fair sized dent in my bonnet. We all piled out of the car to try and catch the bastard who had thrown the brick but were left frustrated as we saw him running down railway tracks on the other side of a wall which was too high for us to drop over and give chase. As we returned to the car which was by now causing a major hold up right into Hartlepool town centre I was once again faced with a repair bill while the others chatted merrily about the days escapades and not for the first time I wondered if it was all worth it.

Another place where we came across some unexpected action was Scunthorpe. Once again we outnumbered the home fans and while there had been a couple of incidents in the town centre before the game, mainly with Leeds fans, we were expecting no opposition in the ground. When we got inside the ground it was pretty much as I had expected. A large group of our lot had already congregated on their kop and the numbers had been swollen by youngsters wanting a bit of glory once they knew the coast was clear. We weren't really interested in unopposed territorial conquests so Jimmy, Dick and me managed to get across to the side terrace where there had been one or two dissenting comments shouted by some Scunthorpe fans in the general direction of our mob. On the terrace it was proving difficult to locate the source of the hostile voices, we must have been spotted coming over as everywhere we looked there were just old men and young kids.

No one was up for it so we decided to go around the back for a pie and Bovril. At the pie stall we came across the first Scunthorpe fans worth bothering with. There were six of them and they had surrounded a couple of our younger lads in the queue for refreshments and were giving it some lip and posing like they wanted some action. They got it, but I wouldn't have called it action. I simply walked up and punched the tallest youth square in the ear hole and all six of them went running off in separate directions leaving me stood in a hole and everyone around looking at me like I was some sort of circus act.

Back on the terrace we stood watching the kop wondering if anything was going to happen and although by now there were a few Scunthorpe fans gathering, they had positioned themselves safely behind a line of coppers and the chance of a scrap looked remote. That was until '*she*' arrived. There was a parting of the crowd near the bottom of the kop and this big fat ugly bird in a long knitted cardigan came stomping through the gap and walked straight into the bottom of our mob. What a Minger she was, she must have fell out of the ugly tree and hit every branch on the way down. Everybody sort of froze wondering what was going on and then backed off in amazement as this monster of a girl started whacking a couple of our skinheads all over the kop.

There was a brief lull in the proceedings as she looked around for more victims and then, as it started to sink in that we were being attacked by a she devil, one lad ran down and smacked her straight in the mouth. Unfortunately for him this was just the point where the police had decided to intervene and he was quickly arrested. I couldn't help but feel sorry for him as I imagined the scene in court where the prosecution described how he had punched a poor defenceless girl, forgetting to say how this girl was something akin to Attila the Hun.

This wasn't quite the end of our escapades though, having found no opposition on one side of the ground we decided to try the opposite terrace and after giving a steward some bullshit about being split up from our mates we were allowed to walk around the pitch to the other side. While this got us where we wanted to be it also alerted the police who then kept a watch on us to see what we were up to. It also alerted a handful of Scunthorpe fans who began to gather around us.

This was what we had hoped for but unfortunately they turned out to be the poorest excuse for a crew that I had ever seen. As the first one gave me a bit of lip I couldn't help laughing in his face which seemed to wind him up a bit. The top boy in this pathetic crew was exactly that, a boy. About eighteen years old, seven stone wet through and built like a survivor from Belsen. What this bunch of tossers hadn't realised was that there were half a dozen boys in blue stood at a discreet distance waiting for something to kick off so they could wade in and have a rumble too.

Coppers loved a ruck just as much as we did and they had the benefit of knowing that while they might get the odd bruise they weren't going to get arrested and locked up afterwards. We didn't have this immunity so we had to restrain ourselves and wait for the right opportunity. The skinny little tosser from Scunthorpe must have taken our reluctance to have a go as a sign of weakness because he started getting more mouthy and their group moved in tight around us. Even then there was no sign that they had the bottle to start throwing any punches. After a couple of minutes of this stand-off I got fed up of the lip and so I decided to try something different. Right in the middle of yet another load of verbals from this wanker I interrupted him and said "Shut up and give us a kiss."

This threw him completely and as he stood there trying to get his head round what was going on I quite slowly raised my right hand and poked my index finger right into his eye. It must have gone in right up to the first knuckle and there was a funny crunching sound followed by a load of pathetic wailing as he bounced, screaming around the terrace until two coppers waded in and carted him away.

As the laws attention turned to this idiot I called to his mates and invited them round the back of the terrace and headed for the toilet block followed by Jimmy and Dick. We were quickly followed by six Scunthorpe lads who turned and did a runner as soon as we made a move towards them. Never mind at least we had some fun.

Chapter 16

BOWING OUT

Darlington 0 – 2 Blades
15th May 1982

Portsmouth 4 – 1 Blades
20th August 1982

Lincoln 3 – 0 Blades
20th September 1982

While being condemned to the Fourth Division might seem to most football fans like the end of the world there were positive points some of which are described previously. The real positive though is that while we were bad enough to get relegated to this level we were, after a change of chairman and manager, streets ahead of everything in the division and we absolutely pissed it.

Also, because we were winning virtually every week, the support actually grew and away matches were like carnivals. The pinnacle of the whole season was when we secured the title at Darlington on the final day. The official figures put the attendance at 11,000 plus. 10,000 being visiting fans but I and thousands of others got in for free by jumping a wall and running across a cricket pitch and were therefore not counted. I reckon there were closer to fifteen thousand people in there and only a thousand were locals. The place was heaving, fans sat right up to the touchlines having abandoned the crush on the terraces. Fancy dress parades and congas took place on and around the pitch before, during and after the game and the handful of Middlesbrough fans that had shown up looking for a fight got the shit kicked out of them and fucked off home early doors.

We had stopped on the way up in Catterick village and played football in and around the stream that runs through the village green. Darlington had been drunk dry and the football match was an irrelevance that was played and won in the middle of the biggest party I have ever seen. There will never be a day like it again no matter how high my team ever reaches and I am proud to be able to say I was there.

After that everything began to change. I was getting older and maybe wiser. Anyway around the start of the following season I discovered I was soon to be a father and suddenly life was different. I had responsibilities now, other people depended on me. People who I couldn't support if I was locked up or crippled through scrapping at football.

The whole football scene was changing too. The media had gone mad, sensationalising what I thought were relatively minor incidents. This stirred up more trouble attracting a different breed to games. Political activists who were trying to stir up anarchy and rebellion against Thatcher's Britain began to get mixed up with football and that wasn't my scene.

While things were changing I didn't suddenly stop; indeed the first game of the following season was away to Portsmouth who were no mugs themselves. We were supposed to go down on the train but on the Saturday morning discovered it was full so we jumped in my car and dashed down to Portsmouth just in time for the game. After the match, which we lost 4-1 we returned to the car to find it surrounded by Portsmouth fans. Heavily outnumbered we went into a corner shop and bought large bottles of pop. After pouring most of the drink down the drains we ran at the Pompey mob with the bottles and they legged it giving us enough time to get in the car and make our escape.

We also had a good run in at Lincoln of all places, we were expecting no opposition but on the run up to a night match in September they put up as good a show as I had seen anywhere for a long time, we had them in the end but it was no cake walk and they earned a lot of respect that night. Other than that there were no real highlights and that season the glamour started to wear off and I found myself getting less involved. I was still there when needed but I found I wasn't really looking for the action anymore. If action came I stood firm and gave it a go but to be honest no team in that division had the bottle to take us on at home and I reduced the number of away games I went to due to my new responsibilities so the action was sparse.

The following year brought promotion to Division Two and that brought a better class of opposition, the likes of Wolves, Leeds, Birmingham and Man City were in the division and the last two came and had a good go and I was always there to help defend our turf. Birmingham became a respected opponent with some spectacular run ins and The Guvnors always showed but always got run, but things were not the same for me. Birmingham were the first crew to bring flares to our place and, while it looked spectacular as they loosed off a few rounds as we ran them through the city centre, for me it marked the beginning of the end. I had always liked the hand to hand stuff, often outnumbered, there was a sense of achievement when you had the opposition on their toes and there was rarely any real damage done. Now there were fifty to a hundred strong mobs of youths, most of whom would shit themselves one on one, throwing missiles and shooting flares in areas where *'civilians'* were going about their business. There was more segregation, the police were getting wiser but as the police got smarter so did the thugs. Fights were arranged outside towns by phone. (In later years these arrangements started to be made over the internet) and the spontaneity was lost.

The police reacted again and put more resources into the battle and dawn raids, court cases and prison sentences were making the news. More flares and other weapons started to appear. As more incidents got on the television, and more media people were rumoured to be instigating trouble for stories to report, more idiots started getting involved for their fifteen minutes of fame. It became an escalating spiral, each side feeding off the other while the TV and press photographers were always conveniently on hand to film and report it and further sensationalise the trouble.

The loose rules that most of my generation had stuck to went out of the window. It seemed that everyone and everything was now fair game and to me that was not what it had been about. I had by then totally lost my appetite for it and wanted to make my withdrawal. I was not prepared to be manipulated and wanted no part of the media circus that it was becoming.

There were also the Trendies who came along. I'm not saying these lads weren't up for it, the B.B.C (Blades Business Crew) as they became known ended up a much better and more respected outfit in pure hooligan terms than the Barmy Army ever were but the terraces seemed to be turning into fucking fashion parades. Apparently if you did not wear Stone Island gear, or other such overpriced junk, you weren't worthy. What the fuck was that all about. In my day the last thing you did was wear your best clothes for a punch up. There was every chance you were going to end up rolling about on the terrace with some twat jumping on you. You didn't want to be worrying that your £100 jumper might get a bit dirty. Fuck me what next mascara and nail varnish? No if that was the way it was going the new generation were welcome to it.

186

What really did it for me though was the sudden rude awakening I got one Saturday morning while shopping down town. Bradford City were due in town and about a hundred of them had come in really early before the pubs were open. I heard them shouting and bawling in the hole in the road (a pedestrian subway that used to be in the centre of Sheffield) and made a bee line for them. There I was, on my own, with a carrier bag full of clothes and I found myself running to confront a hundred rowdy Bradford fans single handed in a fucking subway. What was that all about? Fortunately something in my head clicked and said 'What the fuck are you doing,' and I turned away went home and never really went to football looking for trouble again.

It had started out as fun, a few kicks, a lot of laughs along the way, but it was always between willing rivals where those who wanted it got it, those who wanted to watch it (and there were always plenty of those) stood on the side lines and basked in the reflected glory as their lads ran the opposition. Those who wanted nothing to do with it stood somewhere else and generally remained unmolested. Now it seemed there were no rules, no boundaries, and no honour and I was in danger of going the same way. Well sorry but no.

Looking back on it now all I can do is ask myself a few questions:

Am I ashamed of what I was? - No. At the time that *was* me and I've never being ashamed of being me.

Am I proud of what I was? - Not particularly. Some people will identify with me; some will think I am scum. I don't mind either way. I don't boast of my past but I am not going to deny it either.

Did I learn anything from it? - Oh yes

What I did, what I was, defined me as what I am today. That may sound strange given the context of this story but I feel it made me a stronger person. It gave me confidence, it made me proud; it made me loyal towards those who show me loyalty. It made me dangerous to those who threaten me or my people.

I learned tactics and planning, I learned some psychology, I learned about others and I learned about myself. I learned to stand up for what I believe in and I eventually learned to walk away.

Any regrets? - Of course, but very few; I can sleep at night. I generally played by the rules. I had some good times, met some good people and did nothing that might give me nightmares as I grow old. Looking back now the only real regret is that I never took a camera. I would have loved to have had the pictures, the lasting reminders, the evidence of those crazy, fun days and that *'Barmy Army'*.

Other books by Alan Allsop

You Fill Up My Senses

Following his journey of well over fifty years of following Sheffield United, Alan Allsop describes the rollercoaster ride of emotions that the Blades have put him through as a lifelong fan. From the days of Woodward and Currie, through all four divisions of the Football League and cumulating in promotion back to the Premier League under Chris Wilder. In between there has been a journey that has seen eight relegations, eight promotions, eight unsuccessful play-off competitions, six cup semi-finals, patches of brilliance and periods of mediocrity. There has been drama and controversy, joy and despair, the sublime and the ridiculous; promotions won by the narrowest of margins and relegations sealed by virtually the last kick of the game. Featuring commentary, humour and opinion the book will provide many memories for older fans and perhaps an insight for the younger ones into why the average Blades fan remains such a pessimist.

You Couldn't Make it Up

When Alan Allsop started work as an Apprentice Plumber back in 1976 he expected working life to be hard, serious and anything but fun. However, 27 years of working for Sheffield City Council's Works Department turned out to be just the opposite. In this amusing recollection of working life, Alan describes the reality of working for a large bureaucratic organisation from his humble beginnings as a £19 per week apprentice to becoming a Contract's Manager overseeing a budget in the millions. The scams, the antics and the characters he came across as he rose through the ranks are recalled in detail here in this story. Parts of this tale may seem strange, crazy, even absurd, but as Alan found out as he worked his way up, no matter how bizarre some of the situations he came across may sound.
You just couldn't make it up.

The Soundtrack of an Ordinary Life

Do you ever hear an old song and are immediately reminded of a time from your past? Of course you do; we all do.

Spurred by his own musical reminders, Alan Allsop tells the story of his life. Childhood innocence; teenage angst; overcoming bullying; dreams achieved; dreams shattered; joy and tragedy, fun and fears. A whole range of emotions over the best part of sixty years are laid out here. The various strands of his life: love, family, career and a lifelong dedication to following Sheffield United are bound together by the underlying humour that helped him through it.

Punctuated by references to around 700 songs that trigger the memories, the ups and downs of life's rollercoaster are detailed here in Alan's own forthright style.

With something for everyone to relate to, and ponder over, Alan tells it how it was for him.

An ordinary life?...........You decide.

Twisted Psyche

Not for the faint hearted or overly sensitive and with more than the occasional expletive, Alan Allsop pulls together a collection of verse written over a period of more than thirty years as the school of hard knocks taught him that life is not always easy.

Do not expect poems in the style of Wordsworth, Shelly or Byron. Alan writes in the same down to earth, often hard hitting style with which he has lived his life.

With no punches pulled and often driven by a range of strong emotions, Alan exposes his tormented inner psyche as life tried and failed to knock him down.

While some of the pieces are dark, even when he was writing the darkest of pieces he was usually smiling, if somewhat sardonically, inside. That's the way he is, that's what keeps him going and that underlying humour occasionally peeps through.

Search 'Alan Allsop' on Amazon.co.uk

Printed in Great Britain
by Amazon